T0098697

# Nathan's FAMOUS
## The First 100 Years

# Nathan's
# FAMOUS

## The First 100 Years
### AN UNAUTHORIZED VIEW OF AMERICA'S FAVORITE FRANKFURTER COMPANY

## WILLIAM HANDWERKER
FORMER COMPANY EXECUTIVE
& FOUNDER'S GRANDSON

— WITH —

### Jayne A. Pearl

New York

# Nathan's FAMOUS
## The First 100 Years
### AN UNAUTHORIZED VIEW OF AMERICA'S FAVORITE FRANKFURTER COMPANY

© 2016 WILLIAM HANDWERKER .

All rights reserved. No portion of this book may be reproduced, stored in a retrieval system, or transmitted in any form or by any means—electronic, mechanical, photocopy, recording, scanning, or other—except for brief quotations in critical reviews or articles, without the prior written permission of the publisher.

Published in New York, New York, by Morgan James Publishing. Morgan James and The Entrepreneurial Publisher are trademarks of Morgan James, LLC. www.MorganJamesPublishing.com

The Morgan James Speakers Group can bring authors to your live event. For more information or to book an event visit The Morgan James Speakers Group at www.TheMorganJamesSpeakersGroup.com.

**Shelfie**

A **free** eBook edition is available
with the purchase of this print book.

CLEARLY PRINT YOUR NAME ABOVE IN UPPER CASE

**Instructions to claim your free eBook edition:**
1. Download the Shelfie app for Android or iOS
2. Write your name in **UPPER CASE** above
3. Use the Shelfie app to submit a photo
4. Download your eBook to any device

ISBN 978-1-63047-934-3 paperback
ISBN 978-1-63047-935-0 eBook
ISBN 978-1-63047-936-7 hardcover
Library of Congress Control Number:
2016900203

**Front Cover Sign Photo Credit:**
Bill Mitchell Photography

**Cover Design by:**
Rachel Lopez
www.r2cdesign.com

**Interior Design by:**
Bonnie Bushman
The Whole Caboodle Graphic Design

In an effort to support local communities and raise awareness and funds, Morgan James Publishing donates a percentage of all book sales for the life of each book to Habitat for Humanity Peninsula and Greater Williamsburg.

Get involved today, visit
www.MorganJamesBuilds.com

**Habitat**
**for Humanity®**
Peninsula and
Greater Williamsburg
Building Partner

# Dedication

In memory of my late grandparents, Nathan and Ida Handwerker, who founded Nathan's Famous, and my late parents, Murray and Dorothy Handwerker, who nurtured the company's growth.

To my wife, Amy, who has always encouraged me to do the things I wanted to do. It was her guidance in expressing my thoughts, memories, and feelings through this emotional journey that brought this book to life with a clearer message to all of my readers.

To my children, Adam and Michael, to my grandchildren Emma and Max and to the generations to follow, so they may have some understanding of their family roots.

To all the employees that worked for my grandfather and father at Nathan's during these one hundred years who also made the journey possible. I would also like to acknowledge the Nathan's employee family that I grew up with as a child and worked with as an adult that are not specifically mentioned by name.

All these people were instrumental in making me the man I am today.

# Table of Contents

# Author's Note

This book reflects my personal views and journey through life and my work years at Nathan's. The book is not authorized by and does not reflect the views of the company past or present.

# Acknowledgments

I have been threatening to write this story since I was just thirteen years old and I first came home from working at the Coney Island store. I distinctly remember telling my mom and dad that I had to write a book about my family, and all that I experienced working for the family business.

I had no illusion that I could write this book on my own. I had asked many, many people for references for someone who could help me to write this book. Amy and I were having dinner with a friend, and I explained that I was writing the story of my family and needed some help in getting this project together. He recommended Jayne Pearl, a writer he's known for many years. I called her and arranged to meet, and we clicked. Jayne was instrumental in helping with the organization of my story. She also helped me power through the emotional parts and tell them in a clear and dignified manner. Those were tough times in this process, and I thank Jayne for her guidance.

I also want to thank the few select people with whom I shared the initial drafts of the book for their feedback to hear what they had to say about the story and how I was going to present it to the public. I listened to all of their comments, many of which helped clarify the message.

Again, I must state that the most valuable guidance came from my family. Amy was instrumental in bringing to the surface my innermost thoughts and feelings once I had developed the storyline. I deeply thank my children Michael, Adam and Franny, Adam's wife, for their comments and for helping me to express many important issues throughout the book. My family continuously supported me to keep the message on track.

I have chosen to acknowledge a quote from one of the world's most famous humble personalities, Mother Teresa. She compiled several statements in one observation on the meaning of life. When I read this passage I felt that it summed up what my family forefathers gave to and took from life. It also epitomizes my views on life and I wanted to share it with everyone. If you take away one thing from your time with me, try and hear her most valuable lessons on how to experience your time on our planet.

Life is an opportunity, benefit from it.
Life is beauty, admire it.
Life is a dream, realize it.
Life is a challenge, meet it.
Life is a duty, complete it.
Life is a game, play it.
Life is a promise, fulfill it.
Life is sorrow, overcome it.
Life is a song, sing it.
Life is a struggle, accept it.
Life is a tragedy, confront it.
Life is an adventure, dare it.
Life is luck, make it.
Life is life, fight for it.
—Mother Teresa

# Introduction

Nathan's Famous started as a New York institution and spread across the country and eventually the world. A small idea, executed at a high level, created a legacy that has carried on for a century. Who would think hot dogs would become one of "the culinary symbols of American democracy"? This was one of my father's favorite sayings, and it reflects the results of my grandparents' hard work and understanding of the basic needs of all ranks of our great country's population.

The birth of the international company began with Nathan Handwerker's struggle to emigrate from Galicia, Poland, to the United States in 1912 at the age of twenty. After arriving in New York, he knew the American dream was alive and well. But it wasn't a flash of lightning or an overnight plan that propelled him to frankfurter royalty. It was his entrepreneurial launch of a humble hot dog stand with his wife, Ida, which planted the seeds that blossomed into one of the largest frankfurter companies in the world.

Nathan and Ida were my grandparents. Their recipe for success was simple: to sell high-quality food items at a fair price. That basic yet welcomed operating principle was the foundation for the entire family business. Over the years, Nathan's Famous was recognized around the world and eventually became a household name. It is a name I am proud of and a family I am thankful to have

*Nathan and Ida Handwerker, circa 1918-21, Brooklyn, NY*
*Photo credit: Handwerker Family collection*

learned from. My grandparents' legacy is something I am honored not only to be a part of but also to be able to share with you.

As my grandfather liked to say, Nathan's has grown "From a Hot Dog to a national habit."[1] As the company expanded beyond Coney Island, my father, Murray, revamped the marketing phrase to "From a Hot Dog to an Inter-national Habit." By most estimates, Nathan's has sold billions of hot dogs, bringing smiling faces to the people. Some may say we are in the frankfurter business, but I say we are in the business of making people happy. Our delivery mechanism just comes on a warm bun.

---

1   This company slogan, developed by Nathan in the 1950s, initially read, "From a Hot Dog to a national habit." Sometime later in that decade my father inserted the word "inter" before the word "national."

My grandfather had very strong beliefs on many levels. In fact, one of his basic philosophies was imparted to me at an early age. His mantra was to sell the highest quality product possible, which translated even to the name of that product. Heaven forbid he ever heard anyone call his product a "hot dog." If they did, he would quickly remind them: "You should never call them hot dogs. Hot dogs are made from inferior meats. Nathan's frankfurters are made from all beef and a special spice formula!"

If you even spoke that widely accepted description, he would make you feel like you uttered a four-letter word. Although I called them franks for many years to come, it was futile to fight common parlance in pop culture, and even he eventually relented. And so, in our company's culture, the hot dog generation was born.

The family business was in my blood even before I began to work with my grandfather and father. From as early as I can remember, I wanted to work next to my father at Nathan's and learn everything he did so I could one day help run the business. Nathan's was "it" for me. I didn't want to do anything else. I was proud of what we built and was dedicated to continuing the quality of our family business. It was in my mind and in my blood to build a great company for generations of Handwerker families.

When I turned thirteen, my wish came true. While I was upset that it took so long for my parents to allow me to become part of the family business, I was overwhelmed with joy and excitement from day one. I worked throughout all of my school years until I finished college. Then in 1976 I began working full-time at Nathan's after graduating college. I was part of Nathan's Famous daily operations during the next twenty years, and even after my father sold the company in 1987.

My father taught me—and I remain a strong believer—that you have to get up-front and personal with the nitty-gritty operations of your company to fully understand successful business strategies. You should work to obtain personal knowledge of the "true experience" of your employees and customers on a day-to-day basis to understand the nuts and bolts of your company. I am indebted to my dad for allowing me the opportunity to follow this philosophy.

Over the course of almost thirty years, I observed the company from many vantage points, as I worked in different restaurant locations and management positions, from opening the Coney Island front counter as a young adult to marketing, purchasing, and finally to corporate food service for the company. My ringside seat provided me with insights into how and why the company experienced spurts of growth while simultaneously surviving shifting winds during inevitable setbacks. Working in the family business presents an entirely unique set of obstacles and challenges.

Behind the scenes, I heard earfuls of beneficial strategic discussions and witnessed occasional disagreements among family members and management. But through a common desire to build a legacy, and our love for one another, we found ways to overcome the nonsense and set aside the family drama to move toward the common goal.

Having grown up during a time when our family, its business, and Coney Island itself were in constant transformation, I am positioned to present my firsthand observations and perspectives of exactly what transpired. Throughout the forthcoming pages, I reflect on the company's rickety ride through intermittent tenuous success, its glorious heyday, and all the ups and downs in between, against a backdrop of ever-shifting economic, cultural, regulatory, and political issues thrown our way.

My sources include personal memories and conversations I had with my grandparents and parents, who never tired of discussing the early years and different business situations or marketing campaigns, as well as how we might expand the Nathan's concept. More recently, I conducted interviews with longtime employees, friends, and acquaintances integral to the company's development. I dug up and sifted through countless documents, correspondences, personal pictures, and media accounts about various family and business milestones to ensure the information herein is accurate.

Another crucial resource includes the hours of interviews my cousin David Sternshein conducted with our grandfather, Nathan, just months before his death in 1974 at age eighty-one—may his memory be a blessing. Those tapes reveal a spirited, tough businessman who was determined not to allow his family to suffer the kind of deprivation or degradation he experienced while growing up poor in "the old country."

These lessons from a hard-nosed immigrant taught me more than I could ever learn from textbooks or academic settings. I am a product of my years with Nathan's Famous. I am even more confident that the lessons I learned from my grandfather and father, and from working within the family business, could be extremely valuable and meaningful to anyone starting a new company or looking to grow an existing one.

All of these experiences have enabled me to take a step back and contemplate the history and legacy of my family and our little frankfurter business. The story of Nathan's Famous (and our family) has many twists and turns. My account may sometimes feel like a Coney Island ride—often a wicked fast rollercoaster, sometimes the thrilling Steeplechase, or a revolving carousel with floating wooden steeds and music of the calliope playing. The ride will be worthwhile and provide many practical benefits, as well as a great account of Nathan's Famous.

If you've never been to Coney Island, this book is bound to serve as a sensory smorgasbord, bringing you the scents, sounds, and most of all, the flavors surrounding Surf and Stillwell Avenues just off the Boardwalk through the unique lens of the Nathan's Famous story.

Preserving this legacy of hard work, spirit of entrepreneurship, and perseverance comprises the first purpose of this book. I am proud to be part of the heritage that continues to give pleasure to those who stop by the original location and the many Nathan's restaurants around the world, as well as those who purchase Nathan's products to prepare in their own homes.

Second, this book culls the lessons from my grandfather, who built something out of nothing with the sheer force of grit, self-sacrifice, and determination; from my father, Murray, who had the passion and vision to expand the company's menu and its geographic reach around the world; and from various mentors who helped my father and me to achieve those goals. Our hard work should inspire readers who have the passion, grit, and willingness to roll up their sleeves and open their own proverbial hot dog stands.

Many of my stories will inform as well as entertain readers. These lessons have also served me well in my work and life, and they serve as an important slice of my family's legacy—a slice I am confident will inspire you throughout your journey.

Within these pages, I have tried to present the stories of this journey in an honest and balanced way. As a result, I hope and intend that my book will help keep current and future generations of my family feeling proud, while inspiring nonfamily readers to remember, reflect on, and relate to their own rich heritage.

Have fun reading my book, and try eating a good frankfurter every now and then. Better yet, plan a trip to Coney Island and stand in front of the original Nathan's Famous on the corner of Surf and Stillwell on a hot summer day. Then take a deep breath to enjoy the combination of smells of salty ocean air, fresh grilled hot dogs from the many full grills behind te counters, and our beloved fresh-cut crinkle french fries. Your mouth should start to water in anticipation of that first bite into the frank as it snaps and the juices explode with flavor.

But a word to the wise: when you order your first frankfurter, take a bite without slathering anything on it, to enjoy what the best frank in the world tastes like. To quote my father, "The best way to take your first bite of a Nathan's hot dog is to have it *au natural*. Then put on either mustard, ketchup, or whatever toppings as you like." The memory should last with you forever!

## Section 1

# FROM STEAMSHIP
# TO ROLLERCOASTER
## 1882 - 1940's

*Nathan (in front of counter with tie and coat) working
at Max's Busy Bee, Manhattan, NY. 1914-1915
Photo credit: Handwerker Family collection*

## Chapter 1

# From Galicia to Manhattan

## The End of an Era

**O**n March 23, 1974, almost three years after Nathan and Ida Handwerker retired, Nathan suffered a heart attack at his home in Florida and passed away. It was the end of an era. At the time, I was away at Ithaca College. When my mom called to tell me that Grandpa had died, I returned home immediately for the funeral in Brooklyn, NY.

I can remember it like it was yesterday. We drove up to the funeral home where the service was being held, and crowds of people were everywhere. My grandma had already arrived and was sitting in a private room, while the family was waiting to offer the inevitable final tribute that would begin shortly. Walking into that room was a surreal experience. As a teenager I tried to comprehend what was happening and did not know exactly what to think or say. We were all grieving and struck by great sadness.

The chapel was jam-packed with caring people—from longtime friends to business associates and neighborhood people who came to pay their respects to our family. When the funeral director indicated it was time for our family to walk to our seats in the front row, I remember looking back to see an ocean of people. The sun glared through the windows with a blinding burst of light that illuminated the room with patches of brightness. It prevented me from seeing anyone's face, so I was able to simply absorb the moment and become lost in the grief of losing such a wonderful man. At that time, I just wanted to be with my family, and I shut out everyone else's presence. In that moment I came to the realization that the service was about to start.

I cannot remember any of the eulogies offered that morning. But what happened after the spoken words passed still chokes me up to this very day. At the end of the service, Grandma Ida said to my dad, to my uncle, and to my aunt that, before laying Nathan to rest, she wanted to drive him past the Coney Island store for one last trip. I didn't grasp the full power of this request until the funeral procession slowly inched by the Coney Island store. As it passed, all the employees and customers who stood curbside, had their hands placed over their hearts. It was a great and fitting tribute, an intensely emotional moment, and one felt especially by my grandma.

*Nathan's funeral procession passes by the Coney Island store.*
*Photo Credit: GettyImage*

I was amazed to see the looks on the faces of the people standing there in tribute to my grandfather. I was extremely proud of my grandfather and the effect he had on so many people. I'd like to think Nathan would have been thrilled and proud to see how much he was loved and appreciated. He was never one to showboat or brag about himself. He was a tough guy who didn't take any crap. He took great pride in the products he sold, and how they were prepared and served to his customers.

My grandfather gave back to the community on an ongoing basis. From the beginning, he just wanted to give the world a product that made them smile. He took great delight in knowing that a well-prepared frank and an order of french fries could fill the stomachs of our loyal customers and make them feel very satisfied. As dramatic as the end of Nathan's life was, that's how humble its beginning was.

> **Frank Lesson:** *No matter what you do, find joy in it. Direct your actions to secure a purpose that can make a difference in the world around you.*

## Humble Beginnings

In late nineteenth-century Poland, there was a simple recipe for life for the majority of the population: try to get by until the next day, and maintain hope in the process. Such was the case of the Handwerker[2] family of Narol, a town of about five hundred people in Galicia, Austria-Hungary, which today is Poland. That's where Nuchum (who would become known as Nathan after he immigrated to America) was born on June 14, 1892. Nathan was one of thirteen siblings, seven brothers and six sisters (plus three other sisters from Nathan's father's first wife). Their father, Jacob Handwerker, was a shoemaker. Their enterprising mother, Rose, sold vegetables and chickens in an open market in town.

Like most of his contemporaries, Nathan never knew what it was like to be *just* a kid. In fact, he had little time for playing ball or hanging out with friends. As a typical child of the poorest of working families, as well as being the youngest male, when he wasn't working for money he swept and polished the

---

2    Handwerker means craftsman in German, Dutch, and Yiddish.

floor, cleaned buckets of sewage from his home, and washed dishes at the nearby stream, drying them with thick grass near the water.

Clothing was not about fashion; his hand-me-downs were the last stop and not in the best shape after extensive use from his siblings who came before him. However, Nathan was proud of his shoes because, after all, his father was a shoemaker and they were made very well. He took pride in what he had, no matter the surrounding circumstances.

Nathan's childhood years taught him how to persevere through tough physical and mental conditions. The feeling of living in a crowded house with little food and lots of hungry children never left his soul, even after he became more successful than he could ever imagine. As a child and young adult, he always thought about how to do more for the family's survival than for himself. He was obsessed with finding ways to improve his family's situation. That attitude and common goal was a constant throughout his life. Nathan never forgot where he came from, especially after he left. He took great pride in his heritage and always strived to include his family in his success.

Religion was a major part of Nathan's upbringing. Jacob, my great-grandfather, took his responsibility as a Jew seriously. As was customary in religious families, Jacob sent his sons to Hebrew school to begin studying with a local rabbi at the age of three. Nathan continued to study whenever he wasn't hustling for work. Shortly after turning six, he went to synagogue both morning and night to pray. His Jewish heritage remained important throughout his life.

## Nathan's First Jobs

During his years in Poland, Nathan and his family often traveled through many towns to try to find consistent work. That "never give up" attitude propelled him to do whatever was necessary to earn enough money to buy food for the day, even if it meant weeks or months away from home. Although the youngest, Nathan seemed especially driven to do whatever he could to help. He was a team player and worked to carry his weight, even at a young age.

At the age of six, Nathan asked his father to let him go with him to a town a few miles from Narol to look for work. They went into a bakery and arranged for the owner to hire Nathan. While his age and size prevented him from lifting heavy sacks of flour, Nathan was able to take baskets full of fresh, hot knishes to the streets and go door-to-door, singing, "Hot and fresh knishes for sale!" A knish is a Jewish delicacy typically made from potato and onion or *kasha* (buckwheat), wrapped in thin dough, and baked thoroughly. He quickly sold out his inventory every day. There was no doubt his entrepreneurial spirit was embedded within his heart and soul from the beginning.

The owner let Nathan sleep in the bakery, and he fed him daily with more food than Nathan ever ate at home. It may have been that first job in the food industry that inspired his desire to enter the food business later in life. Funny enough, through running a successful food operation, he likely felt confident that his family would never go hungry again. Nathan viewed each job he had as an opportunity to develop, to grow, and to shape his destiny, even if he remained homesick during the process.

I can only imagine how Jacob and Rose felt leaving their six-year-old son in a town a few miles away from home to learn a trade, with no family or support nearby. It's hard to conceive of circumstances so desperate and difficult that Jacob would allow his young son to take the job away from home. I also wonder why Jacob didn't take this menial job himself, instead of leaving his young son in the hands of a stranger. Even though Nathan asked his father to let him have this job, it proved too much for the six-year-old boy.

After just one week, Nathan felt so homesick that he walked home by himself, more than two miles. He must have remembered the route he and his father had walked to get to the nearby village, and simply followed the same way home. It was then that Jacob realized he should train his young boy in his own craft. Upon his return, Jacob started to teach Nathan his profession as a shoemaker. Nathan proved to be quite the cobbler and picked up the trade very well in the years that followed.

When Nathan was only seven or eight years old, and while apprenticing for his father, he also dug potatoes during harvest time at the farm of the wealthiest man (the baron) in Narol. Nathan would bring a loaf of bread with him in the morning and drink some water from a barrel in the field during his workday. His hard work for the baron opened the door to a good contact for Nathan when he grew older.

Until the age of eleven, Nathan continued working unskilled jobs while learning his father's trade. He never attended traditional school, although he did make time for his Hebrew and Torah studies when he was not working. Formal education was never a priority—then or later in his life. Learning how to provide was everything. The Handwerkers recognized that education comes in various shapes and sizes and always welcomed any unique opportunities to learn.

At age eleven, Nathan was ready to find another job, this time in the big city of Radon. He had liked working at the bakery, so he found another one in Radon that immediately hired him. He hadn't returned to his prior employer because he was extremely embarrassed that he left the job after just one week. Now that he was older and stronger, he was able to pick up huge bags of flour to make the dough. The baker would wake him up every midnight to start his work. He slept on a cot at the bakery and worked there for two years, not going home even once. He sent most of the money he earned to his family. Here is an account in his own words about his tasks on this job:

> I had to sift the flour, 180 pounds of flour in each batch. So he gave me a sifter, about 2 feet, maybe about 20 inches diameter. He used to put them into the shuffle, the flour, and I sifted and he mixed it up. Then we took the dough, cut up pieces, and weighed it and worked it out, put it in a big basket to rise. And I had a long table, twice as long as this room, to put on these big baskets…10 pounds…with the dough. When the dough started to rise up to be able to bake, he had the stove heat up to be able to put the bread in. He sat on a big chair to be able to put his feet on; he had to sit up and I had to hand over a basket and turn it over on the shovel, a wooden shovel, and he put it in. And I went back with another basket. By the time I took the basket and I came back from the oven, I fell asleep. When I touched the oven, it's hot. I woke up. Then I turned over the bread to the shovel. Then when all the bread was baked we had to put it in big baskets—10-pound baskets: 30, 40 breads in big paper baskets that I made. We had a long wheel wagon in the front and

two handles in the back. I put the strap on my shoulders and he loaded up the wagon to take the bread out to the town where he had a store to sell it. Every baker, every merchant had a store to be able to sell. So I did that.

During his stay in Radon, Nathan continued to study Torah with a local rabbi. In the Jewish tradition, he became a Bar Mitzvah (the Jewish coming-of-age ceremony) when he turned thirteen years old, celebrated by reading a portion of the Torah in front of the congregation. He had no party with family and friends. He also didn't receive any gifts, yet both are customary in today's society. The only celebration was the event itself and becoming a man in the eyes of God and his community. He then decided it was time for him, as a man, to move on. So once again he decided to return home, as the Jewish holiday of Passover was fast approaching. But before he left he made one stop: to the best butcher in town. He gave the butcher all the money he had saved except the equivalent of ten cents, which he used for a ride home on a horse and wagon.

Nathan wanted to bring home this surprise for his mother and siblings because he knew they had not eaten meat for countless months. He recalled, "It would take too long to walk. I figure if I carry the meat, the meat would get spoiled." His actions revealed his values with little regard for anything special for himself. Nathan recognized that all he had was his family, and he did what he could to provide for them.

When he returned home this time, he decided to stay in his home town and work. He helped his mother, who was now peddling vegetables in town. Whether Jacob was on the road begging, or at home, or even away making shoes, Rose decided to supplement the family income by opening a stand in the local market and selling her farmed goods.

In those days, this was not the normal role of a woman, and she experienced a sexist reaction by some of the peddlers who were not happy that a woman would even think to be a breadwinner. In helping his mother, Nathan recalled his first business deal with the local baron, for whom he had dug potatoes when he was younger. The baron had the most land to grow vegetables and the financial ability, as well as facilities, to store them well beyond the normal seasonal limitations. So when Nathan's mother and the rest of the peddlers ran out of potatoes in July that summer, Nathan had an idea.

He made a deal with a cousin who had a horse and wagon and went to the baron to buy some potatoes from his full warehouse. At the time, potatoes were not a vegetable often seen at the market, so they were coveted and always a quick seller. Nathan wasn't sure the baron remembered him, so he explained that he had dug potatoes on the baron's farm when he was younger. He and his cousin cut a deal for an entire wagon of potatoes. They packed as many 180-pound bags of potatoes as the horse and wagon could carry and went back to town so they could sell them. The family was excited and knew the potatoes would be a welcomed addition.

Rose was a savvy businesswoman. When they returned with the wagon and all the peddlers saw what they were carrying, they each wanted to buy a full bag so they could resell smaller batches for even more money to the general public. She instructed Nathan to sell the farmers no more than 5 to 10 pounds apiece for a much higher price per pound than if she had allowed them each to buy a 180-pound bag.

Rose instinctively understood the concept of wholesale versus retail pricing. As a result of both mother and son's savvy business dealings, the family finally had some money for the summertime. But when Nathan asked his mother if he could go back to the baron and get another wagon full of potatoes with his cousin, she quickly responded that he could not.

Rose was superstitious because Nathan's cousin had already gone back without him. The horse collapsed and died during the return trip. Because of that, Rose believed God punished the cousin for being greedy. She didn't want Nathan to suffer the same fate, so his potato-dealing days were over for the time being. But the lessons he learned as a future businessman had just begun. Nathan secured an opportunity to sell potatoes where others did not and created a successful business endeavor for his family. This was just one example of how his entrepreneurial spirit was quickly growing.

Nathan learned that his mother's business acumen was vast. She understood that the rest of the peddlers were trying to put her out of business by buying all of her bags of potatoes. After that event, the farmers tried to cut her access to other produce by meeting farmers who sold to peddlers and making their deals before she had a chance to negotiate deals of her own. Thus, there would have been nothing left for her to buy when the farmers came to town.

Perhaps the peddlers looked down upon her because she was a woman. Then again, perhaps they felt threatened by her superior business acumen. It didn't matter to Rose. She knew she could outwork and outsmart the competition, rarely looking to them for acceptance or guidance in good business practices.

Undiscouraged, Rose decided to beat the farmers at their own game. She went directly to the farms to meet the farmers before they came to town, cutting the other peddlers out. She would buy whole wagons full of various types of produce such as: carrots, potatoes, horseradish and occasionally she would even buy some chickens. The family rented a cellar in a building in the middle of town to store the vegetables so they could sell them during the rest of the season. Every day they would spread all their goods outside on the ground. At the end of each day, Nathan would haul whatever was left over down to the cellar, only to lug them back up again the next morning to be ready for business.

"I used to carry it down in the dark," Nathan said. "If I had a big sack of potatoes, it would be hard for me to pick it up again. So I had to go down in the dark slow, with a candle. I used to sleep there so people wouldn't steal the food. That was my job. Then I had to go home, sit down on the bench, and make shoes. I did that till I was about nineteen."

Nathan also recalled that he was not allowed to eat a whole pear, only the broken ones. The family would eat the damaged fruits and vegetables and keep the whole ones to sell. He learned much from his mother and father. He knew that he would put those lessons to good use in the future. He only had to get out of his situation and into a position to be successful on his own.

**Frank Lesson:** *Sacrifice personal enjoyment for professional gain. It is the small decisions that can often make the biggest difference.*

## Big Dreams for Young Nathan

The generations that came to America in the past had one thing in mind: creating a better life for themselves and their families. They worked at whatever job they could get, for however many days per week necessary to make ends meet, with the hopes of saving up for the tougher times ahead. They also tried to sponsor relatives from the old country who wanted to emigrate and follow in their footsteps. This was the typical strategy for building a better future.

Many of today's immigrants have the same drive to succeed by taking two or three jobs to feed their families. Their work ethic is just as powerful as my grandfather's. Their diligence and desire to take advantage of opportunities helps to make America great.

It was no different for Nathan. Between the ages of thirteen and nineteen, he not only became highly skilled at making all types of shoes, but he also dreamed of going to America to become successful in business and start a family of his own. He felt determined to transcend his early life circumstances that deprived him and his family of the basic necessities of life.

Nathan's credo was that if you worked hard, nothing should stand in the way of providing proper food and shelter for one's family. It wasn't an easy beginning for the man who I believe opened the first true fast food restaurant in America. If only he had known at the time that one day he would become immortalized for

*Nathan's Famous, Coney Island, circa early 1940s*
*Photo Credit: Nathan's Famous website*

creating a company that provided everyday food products to the masses. Most people who have tasted his namesake, a Nathan's hot dog, agree it is a unique eating experience.

As previously explained my family name means craftsman in German, Dutch and Yiddish. My grandfather embodied the essence of being a craftsman. His workmanship resulted in a 5 cent frankfurter and other menu items that met the taste and price structure of the American consumer. His hard work and marketing skills completed the recipe which enabled him to create his "work of art", a successful business.

In 1912, at the age of twenty, Nathan took the first step toward fulfilling his dream when he traveled to the United States on a ship with hundreds of fellow immigrants. He couldn't afford a first or even a second-class ticket. The vessel had been converted from a cattle transport into a passenger ship, so even the best of cabins weren't anything like the *Queen Mary* accommodations. Traveling third class, he had to share a cabin with six or more people with beds that were stacked up on berths three high.

These lower-class cabins and public areas were a playground for pickpockets and thieves. Nathan said he slept with his shoes on to make sure no one could take his money, which he kept in his socks. He would go on deck every day to take off his shoes and let his feet breathe and his shoes air out from the smell. He always kept his eyes open. Even in business, Nathan knew his competition would always want what they could not have, and would strive to create problems unless he remained focused and aware.

Upon his arrival in America, Nathan was very happy and surprised when one of his relatives came to pick him up at Ellis Island, as Nathan didn't speak a word of English. But like many of his generation who arrived in America, he quickly learned how to survive and to succeed.

## Early Days in America

Nathan found a job with a cobbler in Manhattan on Avenue A and 9th Street on his very first day in America. Before he launched his career in the food industry, he made shoes six or seven days a week. While he made some seemingly counterintuitive decisions in those early days, they were always based on long-term thinking. For instance, he found a job sewing at a luggage factory for $8 a week and then gave up that job to become a dishwasher for $4.50 a week at a luncheonette.

"I didn't want to be a slave in a factory and breathe in the dust every day," he explained. "I had a chance to work my way up to something, to learn something else. I always wanted to be in a restaurant." Nathan always saw the big picture and was willing to make decisions that may have impacted him immediately, but would certainly benefit him in the long run.

He got the dishwasher job by exercising his usual tenacity. After convincing the luggage factory owner to hire him, he bought a Jewish newspaper on Sunday and asked a friend to look through the classified ads. He was told of a job at a luncheonette on 112 Williams Street, in Manhattan's Wall Street district. It took Nathan an hour to walk there, but when he arrived at that address, he couldn't locate a luncheonette. He had no way of knowing it was upstairs.

"So I'm standing there," he said, "and who comes over? A bakery driver. This driver came with a horse and wagon. Holsum Bakery, located on Houston Street, was the bakery. The driver sees a Jewish boy and starts to talk to me in Jewish [Yiddish]. I show him the ad, I ask what time they open? He says they're not going to open today. In Jewish, I say why they advertise if they're not going to be open Sunday? He said they made a mistake. But if you come Monday before 6 o'clock you'll be first. I was there 5 o'clock. I got up 4 o'clock and walked an hour in the dark and found the place because I was there the day before. I see the boss. There were people behind me, but he saw me first."

And so Nathan proudly nabbed his first job as a dishwasher in the food industry. The owner, also named Nathan, assigned my grandfather a nickname, Benny, to avoid confusion. At the end of the first day, Nathan properly cleaned so many dishes with so little soap that he earned his first promotion to busboy. At the end of the first week, his manager, Max, handed him $5. "I said boss, you gave me too much money. So he said I give you a raise. *Danke schein* [German and Yiddish for thank you]. But next week you work on frankfurters. I must have worked about three months on the frankfurters."

Soon after, Max left to open a new restaurant because the owner had sold the restaurant to an inexperienced businessman. But even so, the new manager quickly promoted Nathan to manager of cakes and pies. Nathan carried the attitude that he should always do his best, no matter how menial the job. He saw each opportunity as a steppingstone to reach his ultimate goals.

Because Nathan had to come in at 6 a.m., the new manager gave him keys to the store and delegated a lot of responsibility to my grandfather. This made him very proud of his accomplishments. However, Nathan was not happy working under the new management. So when his former manager, Max, asked Nathan to join him at his new luncheonette, Max's Busy Bee on 18th Street between 5th and 6th Avenue, Nathan did not hesitate to accept the position.

"I didn't even ask how much he would give me," he recalled. "Why? Because I knew he knew the business. And the new boss [at the old place] was originally a tailor. I didn't know how long he'd last. When I worked on 18th Street I think he gave me $7.50 per week. Whatever he gave me, I was satisfied." Nathan trusted that as Max succeeded, he would also succeed. Nathan was quick to tie his cart to the strongest horse. He believed the company you kept often dictated much of your success.

Working for fellow Jews behind the scenes, Nathan was able to communicate with his boss and co-workers in Yiddish. Now that he was to handle the front counter and interact with customers, he had no choice but to learn English via OJT (on-the-job training). But his persistence allowed him to learn the language by simply repeating the orders as they were requested, one client at a time. "One cup of coffee, please" or "One slice of cheesecake, please" were some of the first phrases he learned.

He was dedicated and determined to learn as much as he could each and every day. This enthusiasm enabled him to begin a step by step approach in meeting his long term goal of someday opening his own business. Even competitors who came into Max's to look for laborers began to notice Nathan's operational skills. When a different luncheonette owner offered Nathan a job at a new luncheonette for twice what he was making with Max, Nathan was more concerned with job security and upward mobility than immediate pay. "I said I'm sorry, I'm working and I'm not going to give up my job. Why? I don't know how long he's going to last in business. And this boss I'm working for, if he don't last, he'll open up another place. He'll take me with him." Nathan knew that Max was going to provide him the best long term learning experience to ultimately make his dream come true.

At Max's Busy Bee, they sold boiled frankfurters for three cents, roasted franks for five cents, and drinks for three cents. Nathan progressed quickly and became the best employee at each job he held. Eventually Max made Nathan manager of the restaurant, just six months after Nathan arrived in the USA. They established a great relationship and worked together for four years, until 1916, when Nathan opened his own restaurant in Coney Island. Max was likely proud that his protégé "stepped up to the plate" and succeeded on his own.

While still working for Max, Nathan decided to save money. In 1914, he went to Coney Island to see if he could get a second job at a restaurant on Surf Avenue on the weekends to supplement his weekly income. He landed a job as a roll cutter at Feltman's Beer Garden. His work at Feltman's required long hours, often working until midnight before taking the two-hour trip back to Manhattan to wake up Monday mornings at 6 a.m. to get to Max's Busy Bee.

In those days, hot dog rolls came in a wooden crate and had to be cut open by hand with a knife. Nathan became the best roll cutter at Feltman's, and then, shortly thereafter, the best frankfurter salesman. He told my cousin David, "I saved up for maybe four years. I already had about $450. The first $150 I had in the bank. The bank failed, closed up on me. After that I kept money in the stocking in the back of my door." Nathan's tireless work ethic always fueled his success. He remained ahead of the game through his willingness to outwork the competition.

## The Birth of Nathan's Famous

While saving enough money to open his own business, Nathan simultaneously learned everything he could from Max. Nathan knew the time was right to make a move. My grandfather worked both jobs for two years until he made his big decision to go out on his own. In 1968, in the introduction to a cookbook[3] that my father, Murray, wrote, he mentions that Nathan's struggling show business friends—then singing waiter Eddie Cantor and his long-nosed accompanist

---

3  *Nathan's Famous Hot Dog Cookbook: 150 Recipes from the World-Famous Hot Dog Emporium*, by Murray Handwerker (Gramercy Publishing Company, 1983).

Jimmy Durante—resented working for *bupkis* (Yiddish for almost nothing). They suggested that Nathan open his own place and undercut Feltman's by selling hot dogs for a nickel, half of what Feltman's charged.

Rumors have it that Cantor and Durante lent Nathan his initial startup capital, but my grandfather debunks that notion in the interview tapes my cousin David conducted with him. Still, Cantor and Durante remained huge fans of Nathan and his franks. (See Durante pictured as he accepts the Coney Island Achievement Award from Nathan.)

In any event, his close friends gave Nathan the little push he needed. Nathan always recognized the value of strong friendships. He asked a close friend, Sam, who worked in the same building as the Busy Bee, if he wanted to open a place on Coney Island as his partner. Originally the plan was to open the restaurant only on weekends during the summer to ensure Nathan and Sam could continue

*Nathan and Ida with Jimmy Durante, circa 1950-1960*
*Photo credit: Handwerker family collection*

working the regular weekday jobs. They agreed on the plan and started looking at various locations. They chose the corner of Surf Avenue and Schwiekerts Walk, right in the heart of Coney Island. The original site was five feet wide and eight feet deep. My grandfather understood one thing: location was everything. He recognized that this spot was ideal because of the foot traffic, as well as it being visible to everyone coming off the trolley. So they bought the site for $300, with each partner investing half.

At the time, all the restaurants in Coney Island sold their hot dogs for ten cents, so Nathan and his partner initially did the same (despite the advice of Eddie Cantor and Jimmy Durante). They took in $60 the first weekend. Not bad! Even so, Nathan told Sam, "We can't make a profit at these levels." The problem wasn't only that they had just opened and had no brand awareness, the bigger issue was that they were no different from anyone else on the island. Why should any customer choose them?

Nathan discussed this issue with his partner and cited the success of Max's Busy Bee's practice of selling franks for just five cents in Manhattan as a way to stand out. "Why don't we sell our hot dogs in Coney Island for five cents?" he said. Sam said no and an argument ensued.

> **Frank Lesson:** *Always differentiate yourself from your competitors. Being known as something unique will usually put you ahead of the pack.*

Nathan knew he had to make a change, and he did so in a creative way. One Sunday during that first season, he strategically offered to sell his share to Sam for $100, even though they both put in $150 as equal partners. The sole condition of the deal was that if Sam did not have the $100 by the following Thursday, Sam would have to sell Nathan his own share for the same rate of $100. As Nathan expected, Sam never showed up with the money, so Nathan bought him out for $100. Nathan then owned the whole five-by-eight-foot restaurant for $250 instead of $300.

This "Buy-Sell" arrangement came from an individual with no formal education. But he did have a great work ethic and plenty of *sechel* and *mazel*

(Yiddish terms for "common sense" and "luck"), along with his mother's natural sense for business. The next weekend Nathan began to sell hot dogs for five cents.

My father said Grandpa was concerned that the lower price might be a problem because people would think the only way he could sell the hot dogs for five cents was with franks made from horsemeat and not all beef like Nathan's sold. So Nathan borrowed some doctor's coats and stethoscopes from Coney Island Hospital personnel and put them on some men and had them eat franks in front of his stand. Potential customers said, "If it's good enough for doctors, it has to be good enough for us."

As he expected, sales increased using his marketing ideas of reducing the price and showing that the product was good enough for doctors. Nathan took in much more than even he had anticipated—more than four times ($260) as much as he did when he charged twice the price.

This is likely where Nathan developed a motto he would repeat thousands of times to his future bride-partner, and later to his children and grandchildren (especially me), and to his employees: "Give 'em and let 'em eat." My father told me he understood this to mean that if you give customers the best product at the most moderate price, they will come back again and again. It was Nathan's dedication and appreciation for his customers that pushed him to create and serve a product of the highest quality and the greatest taste.

Because of its sudden growth, the business was extremely busy during the summer. So for the rest of the season, Nathan slept in the stand on Saturday nights. There was no air conditioning in those days, so throngs of people would go to the breezy beach day and night, some even sleeping there for relief from the heat, which kept them coming to the stand for food and refreshments.

It didn't make sense for Nathan to close the stand at the end of each day and return the following morning, just hours later. In fact, his new hot dog stand did so well that he made a bold decision at the end of that first summer. He told Max he was leaving his position at Busy Bee to keep his own restaurant in Coney Island open on a full-time basis. Nathan's time was at such a premium that he had to decide between stability and opportunity. Clearly, he made the right choice.

## Naming the Stand

For the first two years, Nathan did not name his food stand. But he knew it was time to make a change when a woman came to the stand during that second summer demanding to speak to the owner. Nathan came up to her and asked, "How can I help you?" She said she wanted to recommend the hot dog stand to all her friends, but because there was no sign with a name on it, she couldn't explain to them how to find the stand. It was then that he named the company "Nathan's Famous."

My grandfather told my cousin David, "I started to think. I worked for Max's Busy Bee. And if I put Nathan Handwerker on [the sign], Handwerker would be hard to remember. I thought *why can't I do the same thing like Max's Busy Bee?* Nathan's… Nathan's…and I paid three and a half dollars for Nathan's Famous. And I registered it so nobody should be able to copy my name. Not the first year, a couple years later. First I called it Nathan's, then I made the tail [on the sign] and called it Nathan's Famous. And I'm still in business."

Notice he did not name his stand "Nathan's Famous Hot Dogs" or "Nathan's Famous Frankfurters." Just "Nathan's Famous." And what *chutzpah* (Yiddish for in-your-face courage) to call his fledgling company "famous." Yes, the business was growing steadily and gaining popularity, but it was far from the household word or "phenom" it was destined to become. And it surely was not even close to being famous in 1920.

As Nathan's business continued to grow, he did not let success go to his head. He attended to every detail himself. But that proved to be harder and harder with every passing day and every new customer. It wasn't long before his five feet of front counter and eight feet of storage space were not enough to meet the demand.

For instance, a food inspector had made him throw out a 40-quart can of milk that had not been put on ice, because there was no room for an icebox. So he bought a saw, a hammer and nails, and carried them on the trolley to Coney Island. He used the tools to extend the storage space by two feet so he could create a new space to hold the milk containers and the blocks of ice to keep them fresh. Nathan was a problem solver. He was always able to think outside the box and find solutions for difficult obstacles in his path.

In that second decade of the 1900s (much like today), Coney Island was bustling with activity. From the way my grandfather described it, there was a frenetic quality in the air. The coming and going of customers, tourists, and regulars alike added amazing excitement and energy to the little island. Customers included long-settled New Yorkers as well as hordes of newly settled immigrants from all over the world, hungry to make it in the New World, and just as hungry for a delicious and inexpensive meal, which they came to know and expect they could get from the Nathan's stand by the beach.

### Special Deliveries
### These Folks Can't Leave Home Without
### the Best Franks in the World!

- We have air-expressed hot dogs to US servicemen stationed overseas in wartime and peacetime.
- We have shipped our franks to actors such as George Segal, Robert Goulet, and Maximillian Schell, when they were filming on location in exotic countries.
- Movie mogul Jack Warner had regular Nathan's shipments sent to his villa in Cannes, France.
- Princess Grace ordered from our menu to her residence in Monaco before her untimely death.
- Barbra Streisand catered a closing night party for one of her shows from Nathan's, three thousand miles away, in London.
- The Queen Mother and her daughter, Queen Elizabeth II, as well as son-in-law Prince Philip, have ordered Nathan's many times on their yacht, *Britannia*, when berthed in New York Harbor.
- Walter Matthau wanted Nathan's hot dogs served at his funeral, and they were.

## Famous Fans

My grandfather always felt that food, and specifically a well-prepared frank, was commonplace and relatable for everyone. It didn't matter the walk of life or economic background of the customer, as he knew that most everyone loved the comfort that a juicy frank could provide. The list of famous and infamous personalities who graced the Nathan's stand is incredibly long. My father mentioned in his cookbook that when business picked up, he started to hire some help. Murray wrote, "One of the part-timers who came after school was a pretty red-headed teenager named Clara Bowtinelli. A talent scout who frequented the stand noticed her and it wasn't long before she was on her way to Hollywood where she became the glamorous '*It Girl*' of the silent movies, Clara Bow."

My father also describes a handsome Englishman, Archie Leach, who took his lunch breaks at Nathan's almost every day from his job as a stilt-walker for George Tilyou's Steeplechase. He would wear a sandwich board advertising the Steeplechase and, on stilts, walk around Surf Avenue or the Boardwalk.

When he sought Nathan's advice about going to Hollywood, my grandfather told him, "You can't sing, you can't dance, and you're no good at telling jokes. Forget Hollywood. Better keep your job here." Luckily, Archie ignored the advice, went to Hollywood, and became a big star we came to know and love as Cary Grant. Despite the fact that Nathan tried to discourage him, Grant remained enough of a fan of Nathan's hot dogs to send us a telegram expressing his gratitude during one of our company's anniversaries.

Even notorious mobsters such as Bugsy Siegel and Al Capone were regular patrons of Nathan's. Over the years, notables from around the globe have had red hots shipped to them. In one of his *New Yorker* magazine columns, Calvin Trillin described Nathan's franks as "the most quintessentially representative of New York." Perhaps that's why local and national politicians also frequented Nathan's. Many considered it politically expedient during their campaigns to be seen in front of the original Nathan's stand.

Kenny Sutherland, Democrat leader of Coney Island from 1917 until his death in 1954, and a member of the New York State Senate in 1919 and 1920, explained, "It's simple to understand. When you're campaigning for public office you want to meet and greet as many voters as possible, and you find many more of them eating hot dogs than pheasant under glass. If you go to Nathan's, you not only meet the most interesting people but you also get something good to

*William Handwerker, Mayor Rudy Giuliani, and Sen. Daniel Patrick Moynihan*
*at a Coney Island event—about to eat a Nathan's frankfurter*
*Photo credit: Bill Mitchell photography*

eat!"[4] But no matter where you came from, in those days Nathan would treat you with care and respect. If you were a customer of Nathan's, you were like family.

From the beginning, we never knew what famous person might drive up in a limousine to purchase a frank. Whether a patron pulls up in a limo or a sanitation truck, we always serve everyone the same way. My father used to say, "No matter whether you are a personality or a hardworking blue-collar person off the street, the hot dog is the culinary symbol of America."

In the Brooklyn tradition of cutting to the chase, we'd greet everyone with the phrase "How many?" I have personally served politicians and celebrities at special events from Senator Daniel Patrick Moynihan, Mayors Rudy Giuliani and David Dinkins, to TV personality Larry King and movie director Sidney Lumet. And everyone was greeted with the same smile and catchy phrase. There's something magical about the everyday experience of eating a Nathan's hot dog.

---

4   *Nathan's Famous Hot Dog Cookbook: 150 Recipes from the World-Famous Hot Dog Emporium,*
    by Murray Handwerker (Gramercy Publishing Company, 1983).

Thousands and thousands of immigrants came to this country with almost no money, unable to speak English, unable to read or write even in their native tongue, with only fire in their belly and the willingness to work hard—incredibly hard, day and night, seven days a week. They would save every penny they could, until they were able to go out to start a new business and then invest their earnings in their own business. Many were successful and many were not. Nathan Handwerker symbolizes one of the best of this country's immigrant stories.

At Nathan's Famous, family members would pitch in from a young age. Not everyone had what it took to succeed. Not everyone shared the same vision. That would create issues within the family. But starting a family business is a family affair. It takes all hands on deck and a common, dedicated effort to make it work, no matter what the obstacles may be.

Nathan's Famous navigated this country's two world wars, the Depression, and many other economic, political, and cultural changes just fine. In fact, the company had a knack for parlaying all sorts of external crises to its advantage with marketing strategies and luck. This had always been a strength of Nathan and the family. We worked to knock out of the park any curveball thrown our way. As you begin a business, and ultimately expand that business, you'll find trials and tribulations around every corner. But how you respond to the difficult times is what will often support your growth and evolution.

## Chapter 2

# Fireworks & Family

*A*s Nathan's Famous grew, it was not without the usual growing pains and family drama. Right from the start, the family had disagreements, whether over work ethic or management styles. This would seem natural with any family business, but it can be pretty overwhelming and daunting when you actually live through it.

Nathan told the story about how he and his older brother Joe,[5] one of Nathan's first employees, clashed over how to make something as simple as lemonade. Nathan showed Joe how to mix the ingredients in a certain order to ensure that the sugar blended properly. But Joe felt that Nathan was just having an ego issue and ignored the instructions, deciding to make it his own way. When the sugar clumped together, Nathan tried to explain to Joe why he wanted the drink made a certain way. Joe started cursing and spit in Nathan's face. Nathan paid Joe his day's wages and never let him work in the store again. Nathan may have been a

---

5    Not to be confused with Nathan's nephew, Joe Handwerker, who married Nathan's sister Gussie and thereby also became Nathan's brother-in-law, who worked in the company for almost fifty years.

tough boss, but he always gave people the respect they deserved, expecting the same in return, otherwise there would be consequences.

**Frank Lesson:** *Have respect for all personnel, no matter what your position is in your business, boss or worker. Respect the decision of your superior or expect the consequences.*

This incident did not deter Nathan from employing other family members: siblings, cousins, and even his wife to be. He recognized the double-edged sword of mixing business with pleasure, but he remained true and dedicated to inviting his family to be part of his success, if they understood and obeyed his rules.

## A Match Made in Coney Island Heaven

In the early 1900s, Coney Island was a small, well-connected community where almost everyone knew one another. Nathan loved to walk around the local streets to see what was going on with the competition. He had his eye on a woman named Ida who was employed down the block on Surf Avenue and lived in a house with one of Nathan's sisters and a couple of other women. He was so impressed by how hard Ida worked that he asked if she would like a job at his stand. She agreed. It ended up being a great decision for all involved.

Once Ida started at Nathan's, her diligence did not go unnoticed by another of Nathan's sisters, who also worked at the stand. At the time, Nathan had no cash register.

He kept the cash in a box on the front counter and in a safe at days end. His sister was apparently jealous of how fast Ida did her job, and told Nathan that she saw Ida putting "something" in her dress pocket, insinuating she was pocketing change. She

*Nathan's first safe*
*Photo credit: Handwerker*
*Family collection*

told Nathan he should fire her. However, Ida learned she was being accused of stealing even before Nathan had a chance to confront her. She was so angry at the false allegations that she quit and then decided to buy a little food stand of her own for just $50.

"She took a place down the block, and it wasn't worth fifty cents," my grandfather said. "She had the little stand in front of the barbershop." While my grandfather didn't feel that she posed any kind of business threat, he was more concerned that she wasn't around for personal reasons.

Nathan believed Ida wouldn't steal anything, and he wanted her to come back—not just as a worker, but as his wife. He knew that she was angry. So he went to the fruit store across the street and bought two large, unblemished pears: one for himself and one for her. But when he offered Ida the pear, in an angry voice she said, "Give it to your sister. She needs it more than me." Ida always spoke what was on her mind, and that was part of what Nathan loved about her. Nathan explained that he didn't believe the allegations were true and indicated that his sister was jealous of Ida and could never work as well as she did.

He told her he found his sister a different job at another store farther down the block. "She had to make a living," Nathan explained. Even though his sister tried to start trouble, he felt an obligation to make sure that family members were able to make a living. Right or wrong, Nathan always considered the best interests of his family.

Luckily, Ida accepted the pear as a peace offering and returned to work for him. However, Nathan did not propose marriage right away. Perhaps he was shy or doubted that Ida cared enough for him and was afraid she would say no.

Always ready with a plan, Nathan asked his cousin Sam, another family employee, to propose to Ida for him—a far cry from today's common practices! As an incentive, he offered to pay Sam $50 if he could persuade Ida to accept. When Sam returned, Nathan asked, "What did she say?" Nathan recalled Sam answering, 'She says she's going to ask her father and mother.' I said, if she's going to ask her father and mother, it means she agrees. If we are engaged, you'll get your $50."

Nathan made good on his promise and paid Sam in pennies he kept on hand for making change with larger currency. Nathan meant it as a joke, because he didn't have any bills on hand. Sam and Nathan laughed and changed in the coins for dollars at the store later that day.

On July 13, 1918, the two were engaged and set the wedding date for three months later on October 26. The wedding was as unusual as their engagement, and not without incident. Nathan picked the venue, retained the rabbi, and bought and oversaw food preparation. In those days, the bride's family usually paid a dowry and made the wedding arrangements. Perhaps Nathan took charge because he was financially successful, well connected in Coney Island, and a total control freak.

In great detail, Nathan described how he planned the wedding: "I hired a woman, a cook. I went to a butcher and bought fifty chickens. And I bought fish. And the cook, she cooked it; I paid her $40 or $50. And I went to a baker and I bought a sack of flour, a whole box of eggs—a big box which would hold sixteen dozen eggs. I paid him for a day's work and he baked *challah* and big rolls and all kinds of cake, honey cake and—what they call it?—sponge cake and cookies and sweet *babka*. The whole day he was baking for $40 for the whole thing. And oranges, we used to pay a dollar a case. But because of the sickness, it was going $10 a case. And I bought a whole case of oranges for the wedding."

Unfortunately, the wedding did not go as planned due to the terrible flu epidemic that year. "Everybody got sick," Nathan said. Only 125 of the 300 invited were able to come. "And my sisters, they got sick. They had the fever. I had to take them home. After the wedding, the rabbi in charge of overseeing that all the food was kosher noticed there was a lot of food left. He said, "'Mr. Handwerker, what should I do with all this food?' [I said] 'Give it to whoever you want. I was sick and tired and disappointed.'" But in typical Nathan style, he rolled with the punches and took everything in stride.

One of Nathan's favorite Jewish sayings was, "Man makes plans and God laughs." But I can only imagine how crushed my grandfather must have felt after all his careful, elaborate planning and preparations for all the socialites and literary and political luminaries who must have been on their guest list.

While the wedding may have felt like a fiasco, the marriage was certainly not. Nathan and Ida shared a wonderful marriage and partnership. And when they started a family, they raised their kids in the most natural place: behind the counter.

## Nathan and Ida Start a Family

Ida gave birth to their first child, Leah, in 1920. While she never worked at the company, Leah did serve on the board of directors many years later, after the company went public. She had a great New York sense of humor filled with sarcasm, which I remember was very sharp at times.

While my aunt was diminutive in stature, she made up for it through her great wit. On many occasions, my father felt that her insights were helpful to set direction for the company. Leah also played the role of the arbitrator, trying to assist in navigating through any family issues that arose. And there were many over the years.

In 1921, my father, Murray, was born just two blocks away from the stand, at Coney Island Hospital. Brother Sol came along four years later, in 1925. Murray liked to say his playpen was a three-by-three-foot crate, in which hot dog rolls had been delivered and were kept behind the counter. He literally grew up in the restaurant business. In fact, he burned his fingers on some french fries the first time he climbed out. But his parents were not overprotective in the kitchen or with the outside world, and they let the kids wander unaccompanied on the beach and Boardwalk. They were always quick to set boundaries, but never overprotected or coddled the kids. They allowed the children to develop a sense of wonder and discover life without limitation.

My father told my brothers and me about the event that most impacted him as a child while he worked in the store. At the age of nine, one of his jobs was to "board up" frankfurters before bringing them from the kitchen to behind the counter, where they would be placed on the griddle. Wooden boards could each hold sixteen frankfurters. Murray was supposed to fill the boards and then place them in a stainless steel carrying case, which weighed about thirty-five pounds when filled.

One day Murray decided to play a game and see how high he could pile the filled boards. He kept adding new boards until the boards were taller than he was. This was not a good idea. After he added one board too many they toppled over, spilling all over the kitchen! Franks and wooden boards scattered around the prep table and floor.

Terrified that he would be punished, he hid under one of the kitchen counters. When they discovered the mess, Nathan, Ida, and the kitchen staff went crazy looking for him. They screamed out, "We won't punish you, just come out from wherever you are!" Murray emerged, devastated but not punished. Nathan felt everyone should learn from his or her mistakes and then move on.

However, Nathan did punish those that disrespected him by stealing from the business. A counterman who was working the frankfurter station was stealing nickels by cutting a hole in his pants pocket and letting the nickels fall into his shoes. At the end of the day he would have many nickels to take home. Well, Nathan suspected him for many days and couldn't figure out how he was stealing the money. Then he saw him actually put the nickel in his pocket. Instead of confronting the man about what he had seen; Nathan brought out a can of orange drink to restock the drink dispenser. However, instead of pouring the drink in the dispenser he "accidentally" spilled the drink on the employee's pants and shoes! Nathan apologized profusely and insisted that he give the worker a new pair of pants, socks, and shoes. As much as the employee tried to refuse my grandfather's offer, Nathan wouldn't hear of it. The two of them went into the back office to change his clothes, and of course the nickels came pouring out of his shoes and Nathan found the hole in his pants pocket. Nathan fired the man without completely embarrassing him, even if he deserved to be humiliated in front of all the employees.

In the end, both Murray and the employees earned valuable lessons from their mistakes: for Murray, first, don't pile the boards too high! Second, don't worry about getting punished for a mistake. Just correct it and move on—a good lesson for anyone to learn early in life! For all employees: Nathan had his ways of getting his message across, and word spread to all the workers not to make the same mistake of disrespecting Nathan and their job. They would always be treated as a valued person if they just did the job they were expected to do.

Nathan was at the forefront of diversity. He hired employees of all ethnicities and religious backgrounds. He was blind to the differences in appearance or culture. The employees just had to be good hard workers, like he was. He always took care of his employees.

As it was for Nathan and Ida, Coney Island became my father's life. There was always a glimmer in his eyes when he spoke of the store and Coney Island. He felt it was a fabulous place to grow up, even though throughout the years it had a reputation for attracting some less than savory characters. My dad described Coney Island as a "summer paradise for the lower middle class." People would come from all over and rent bungalows—which have now been replaced by high-rise urban renewal apartments.[6]

Nathan often reminisced about the unbelievably unique people he would see while serving up franks by the dozen. Those stories were passed along to my father, who enjoyed his own experience while growing up on the island. There was a side show with a variety of different people who lived and worked in Coney Island for many years. "The people you'd see," Murray would always say. "The sideshow people weren't carnival people, really. Carney people travel from town to town. The people I knew had settled down in Coney Island. Actually, it was like growing up in the United Nations long before the United Nations was even thought of."

As a child, my dad was forbidden to go on the jetties in the ocean but was allowed to walk around the Bowery to the various rides and games. Several of my grandfather's relatives lived and worked in Coney Island. They had a similar entrepreneurial spirit and started many different businesses, including the bumper cars ride next door to the restaurant. Murray said he never remembered getting a single ride for free—even though his aunt owned one of the ride concessions. My father also denied ever sneaking into any of the girly shows, although he did recall visiting Tirzah and her Wine Bath, which a 1966 *New York World-Telegram* article describes "She wore more than the average woman wears on the beach today and her bath was just water colored with some harmless purple dye. There was a lot left to the imagination. Youth is being cheated today. Nothing is left to the imagination."

---

6  "Hot Dog! What a Success," *The New York World-Telegram,* by Hope Johnson, Thursday, March 10, 1966.

Nathan worked twenty hours a day, sometimes seven days a week, and had Ida by his side for most of that time. She managed the kitchen and the children, while endlessly peeling onions and potatoes. No one could slice onions faster than she did. My father liked to recall that she often raced with the other workers—and she always won.

From the start, Ida and Nathan's working relationship grew stronger with every year that passed. As the business grew, the amount of pounds of frankfurters purchased by Nathan's increased tremendously. My dad told me Ida felt that they could and should demand that the manufacturer use Nathan's Famous own special spice formula. Nathan agreed with her and she developed the unique flavor profile that still remains today as the taste that has satisfied millions of people.

The two of them made the most of their time with the kids under the circumstances of the summer business demands. Even with his busy work schedule, Nathan made time to see his kids during the height of the summer season when Murray, Sol, and Leah were away at summer camp in Monticello, about two hours north of New York City. Nathan would close the stand at 3 a.m. whenever he could, drive to be with his kids for breakfast, then drive back to open the stand for rush-hour lunch business.

It was enormously important to my grandfather to spend time with his kids, no matter how brief. He recognized that time was precious, and he did what he could to be a part of their lives. Sharing meals with them allowed meaningful conversations about their summers and their lives. Nathan cherished these moments and loved his children more than anything in the world, a feeling he carried with him throughout his life.

## The Roaring Twenties and Booming Thirties

In the fiftieth anniversary edition of the company newsletter, *Frank-ly Speaking*, my cousin Joe wrote that he started working for the company at age twelve.[7] "This summer, I will be here for 46 years," he reminisced in that article. "I used to work 14 hours or more every day, seven days a week. When I started I was a counterman, kitchen man, and general all-around helper. I peeled potatoes and

---

7    He would have been age twelve in 1920, the company's fourth year of existence.

onions, washed floors, walls, and ceilings, painted, counted money, and did just about everything. Family or not, we all started from the bottom and worked our way up. In 1920 we had about 10 to 15 employees during the summer season. Every year since the time I started—even during the Depression—business got better. From the little eight-foot counter, the Coney Island store has grown to about a square block in size." In the beginning, Joe recalled, the store extended from the corner griddle to eight or ten feet in the front. The kitchen extended through the back of the store. In the late 1920s, Nathan's Famous added a dining room and an upstairs that was furnished and briefly rented as a rooming house until it served as my grandfather's office.

*Handwerker family and employees at Nathan's Coney Island,*
*circa 1922-23. Murray is held in Nathan's arms.*
*Photo Credit: Nathan's Famous website*

My father Murray told me that during the Depression, families would split a hot dog into multiple pieces because they didn't have enough money to buy one for each family member. For just fifteen cents, they could feed a whole family with one hot dog and an order of fries. Business was booming more than ever because people could get a high-quality meal at a low cost. Nathan always felt that feeding the masses would be good business. At a time when it seemed like the world was falling apart, his pricing concept would help folks forget their troubles, even if just for one meal.

Joe also recalled, "During the 1930s, it was so cold in the winter, at times the water lines froze. When we served the customer a drink, it would sometimes freeze in the cup. We used to wear potato sacks on our feet to keep warm.

*Leonard Everett Fisher painting depicting customers coming up to Nathan's stand after a great blizzard before the budka.*
*Photo credit: Leonard Everett Fisher*

Shortly afterwards, the *budka* was built, but we always stayed open—no matter what the weather was like."

Ah, the *budka*. In Polish, it means "birdhouse." But at Nathan's hot dog stand, that's what we called a structure we built in the front of the store for the winter. The *budka* consisted of a row of sliding wooden doors that were four feet from the counter, forming an enclosure, like a porch (or birdhouse), from the end of the counter underneath the vertical Nathan's sign, wrapping around the corner. The natural heat from the grills and maybe one or two gas heater-blowers would protect employees and customers alike from the elements. We would break down the *budka* as soon as the weather warmed up in the spring. We used the *budka* until the 1990s, when we changed the layout so that customers could order inside behind pull-down sectional doors that protected them from the biting weather outside. We also set up tables and chairs inside, near our seafood and deli counters.[8]

While Nathan and Ida were running the flagship hot dog stand during the 1930s, both Murray and Sol began working for the company in their pre-teens,

---

8    That new layout remained until Hurricane Sandy in 2013, when five feet of water flooded the Coney Island store, ruining the entire location. An entirely redesigned and streamlined Nathan's reopened the next year, and business is better than ever.

which was typical for sons of family business owners. They started from the bottom: sweeping floors, running errands, stocking shelves. Then they graduated to working the grills and behind the counters.

Murray met Dorothy Frankel while they both were attending Lincoln High School in Brooklyn. My father always told me he was a "leg man" and that is how my mom caught his attention. He sat in the back of the classroom and when he looked down the aisle he saw two beautiful legs stretched out from under a desk in his row. He knew that this woman was for him at that moment and the relationship began at least in his mind. Fortunately, my mom felt something special about my dad when he asked her out on date. They did court for a while and their relationship developed.

Murray 18, and Dorothy 17 made a bold decision to get married the next year. They scheduled their wedding for December 14th, 1941. On Sunday

*Murray goes to war, with Nathan visibly worried, 1942*
*Photo Credit: Handwerker Family collection*

morning December 7th 1941 Murray and Dorothy were sitting at the counter having breakfast at a local luncheonette when they heard the news about Pearl Harbor. Despite the overwhelming sadness of the prior week's event they were betrothed, as life went on. Murray attended the University of Pennsylvania prior to the war and graduated from New York University when he returned from Europe and the army.

When World War II broke out, both sons were drafted. I have included a photo of my father in his uniform with Nathan and Ida at his side. Nathan looks devastated in the photo, as he envisioned his sons, his legacy, going off to war. He must have been imagining the worst: Murray or Sol—or both—could die. I can only imagine the angst both Ida and Nathan went through every day that Murray and Sol were gone.

Thankfully, both sons came home safe and sound, and eventually they went back to work in the family business. A year later, Nathan fulfilled a promise he had made to himself. If his sons returned safely, he decided he would dedicate a *Sefer Torah* (Kosher Torah scroll) to the community in their honor. When both sons made it back in one piece, Nathan and Ida purchased a scroll for their synagogue. Nathan felt strongly about giving back to his community and recognized that as they supported him, he could support them in return.

Now back at the family business, the brothers' personalities and management styles were so vastly different that they found it difficult to work together. Sol was a numbers person: very capable, but cautious. I do recall Murray stating that it was always very difficult to get Sol to make decisions on even minor issues. That was frustrating for my father and grandfather, who wanted to concentrate on sales, marketing, and basic operations, which often required quick responses to opportunities and problems. Murray was always looking for ways to make the company grow via menu, promotional activity, and the addition of physical store locations, while Nathan always worked to invest his time and energy into the current Coney Island family business. He saw it like a garden that needed constant attention and had to be nurtured in order to grow.

While most of Murray's decisions were positive ones, he had his share of miscalculations. However, make no mistake about it: Murray's hard work and determination to make the company grow resulted in great success for Nathan's

*Nathan and Ida riding in a car
on Ocean Parkway, Brooklyn,
dedicating Sefer Torah
to the community
Photo Credit: Handwerker
Family collection*

Famous. While many of his early efforts met with resistance not only from his brother, but sometimes also from his father, he was never deterred.

## Surreptitious Expansions

During WWII for a period of two and a half years, my father served in Europe as an interpreter in the 225th Searchlight Battalion. He spoke fluent French, German, and was conversational in Russian. He facilitated cooperation between headquarters and the local populations, serving in England, France, Luxembourg, and Germany.

My father told me he had an anti-Semitic captain. While the army was pre-staging the Normandy invasion in England, his division was stationed in an unheated castle. Every room had a fireplace. For three or four days, his captain made him stoke the fires for twenty-four hours a day—taking only catnaps and snacking, unable to eat or sleep with the rest of his division. He knew it was because he was a Jew. When he couldn't take it anymore, he told his story to another captain and got transferred to another division once they confirmed his story.

I cannot imagine that he would ever want to light another fire, but he loved to light fires in the winter. We had a fireplace in our home, and he taught me how to build and stoke a fire, which I still love to do throughout the winters to this day.

During the war my mother also served, in the Signal Corp, as an inspector, SigC Material, CAF-5. From 1943 until she was "demobilized" after V-J Day in

*When can my mother Dorothy be together with Murray again?*

1945 (Victory over Japan Day), she inspected radios manufactured in a facility in Newark, New Jersey, to be used overseas. Dorothy worked, as many women did in those days, to do their part for the war effort.

After WWII, Brooklyn was as vibrant a community as ever. The vets, including Murray and Sol, came home with many different life experiences and new cultural perspectives. Murray realized that, having been exposed to new foods overseas himself, other returning soldiers had also developed more sophisticated tastes and welcomed something new. He wanted to introduce more exotic foods, such as shrimp, lobster, and clams, to Nathan's menu. While one of his father's fears was that adding shellfish would alienate many of their Jewish customers, he didn't stand in the way. He always looked for an opportunity to be innovative, recognizing that this was the quickest way to evolve.

Starting in the late 1940s, Nathan and Ida would go down to Florida every winter. Initially, Nathan was dead-set against selling anything except the basic menu of frankfurters, hamburgers, french fries, and drinks. He would have nothing to do with the planning or execution of any new menu items, but he told Murray: "Do the job when I am in Florida, and don't call me with any issues."

Sol probably did not have a problem with Murray's desire to add to the menu. But getting him to sign off on big, out-of-the box decisions was not within his comfort zone.

In 1949, when Nathan went to Florida for the winter, Murray planned and completed the construction of a new seafood section in the middle of the restaurant. Financially, it was a huge success, but it did complicate the operation. On the plus side, you could not get finer food if you were at any seafood restaurant. Our menu was as freshly prepared as any high-end "sit-down" white-linen restaurant in New York. But in the 1950s the latter would charge a lot more for a filet of fish dish than for filets that we prepared the same way.

When we sold fish filet, it was fresh cod or flounder, always prepared daily. We never sacrificed quality in any capacity. Obviously, customers were not getting the same service or ambiance as they would get at a fancier sit-down establishment with tablecloth service, but they did get a tremendous bargain. Even with the seafood business, Nathan's always strived to serve a quality product for a good value.

On the other hand, from an operating standpoint, compared with making burgers, handling fresh seafood is much more complicated and time consuming. Fish and clams were always delivered fresh and prepared for daily sales. The shelf life of the prepared filets is much shorter and requires much more labor than dealing with whole cuts of meat. In those days, we would grind fresh pieces of beef to make the burgers on different days of the week, but always as needed. We also sold a barbecue sandwich made with a fresh cut of pork, as well as top round roast beef for a roast beef sandwich, both of which would be cooked fresh in the store as needed.

However, specifications called for employees to re-bread the fish and shrimp every day if there were any leftover pieces from the day before, which obviously required additional labor. The employee in charge of cutting the whole filets into portions always had trimmings of the fish that were still edible but not good enough for a portion of their own. So we would accumulate the trimmings from all the whole filets and make fish cakes a couple of times per week as a special menu item. This allowed us to create sales from fish filet trimmings that would otherwise be discarded. They also tasted great and were welcomed by the customers as a special menu item.

> **Frank Lesson:** *Innovation requires out-of-the-box thinking. When life gives you fish scraps, make fishcakes.*

When we started offering seafood, we had to have separate refrigeration and preparation areas from the fresh meat, to ensure we met all menu production requirements. This involved much more time than taking a hot dog from the refrigerator to the grill and then serving it. While seafood cost more, it produced a higher gross profit for every order sold. In addition, selling seafood provided a family or group of friends another reason to come to the restaurant. If one person wanted frankfurters and another wanted fish or seafood, Nathan's could satisfy them both. The quality of the food was never in question.

A few years later, in the late 1950s, when Murray wanted to add a line of delicatessen foods, Nathan initially balked again. So Murray waited for Nathan and Ida to head south for the winter to add the line of deli items that included barbecue chicken, corned beef, pastrami, tongue, turkey, and salads. Like seafood, the deli was a big hit.

At this point, deli and seafood preparations took over the center of the store. More menu items required more space to store the multitude of new ingredients. The stand was bursting at the seams with the sales and production needs of the newly expanded menu offerings. As Nathan expanded his own store, he realized the exciting investment opportunities in and around Coney Island. With his growing familiarity with the land, he began buying up properties near the Boardwalk and building a real estate portfolio.

## Buying Up Boardwalk and Surf

Nathan would buy additional lots on the block whenever he could. He accumulated the entire square block on Surf and Stillwell between Schweikerts Walk and Stillwell Avenue, and Surf Avenue and the Bowery.

While we aren't entirely sure of what Nathan bought and when he purchased property, it was clear from the interview tapes that my grandfather enjoyed buying real estate. Nathan did not explain exactly how he used all of the buildings, but it appears some were used as warehouses for the growing business, while others were rented to businesses or residences. But it is certain that as Nathan's started expanding its menu and the clientele grew, Nathan's Famous required the entire square block on which it was located to serve its customers properly.

Furthermore, Nathan purchased other properties in and around Coney Island, probably to store the ingredients for the growing volume of food they were selling. My oldest brother Steve recalls that Nathan had confidence in real estate investing. He was convinced that it was the best use of the money that the family earned. During a conversation before we went public in 1968, he told Steve, "If it was up to me I would buy every piece of property in Coney Island and never open another store. We [as a family] could make more money doing this than opening any new stores!"

His idea, in conjunction with Murray's expansion efforts, would have proved prophetic. After we went public in 1968, if we only had bought more property, Nathan could have been the largest landowner in Coney Island for pennies on the dollar. But then again, hindsight is a wonderful thing in business. If we only knew then what we know now!

My grandmother was not as enthusiastic about the property purchases, and she ultimately retained a lot of influence about investing more money in Coney Island. My father told me that Ida and Nathan would argue about buying new properties. Ida said, "Nathan! Enough!" I was told of one example when, in the mid-1950s, Nathan was offered the Queen's Plaza site, right in the middle of Queen's Boulevard, which is now home to a huge mall. That's when Ida put her foot down and told her husband, "Nathan, we have enough property." Unfortunately, they never bought that site, effectively ending their real estate acquisition days.

But it was through this vision and understanding of investments that Nathan showed exactly how knowledgeable he was not only in real estate, but also in how to select assets and make them grow through wise business decisions. However, his marriage to Ida and her ideas trumped investing more money in real estate than he already had in Coney Island or anywhere else.

## Growing Pains

The menu additions not only required more real estate space, but they also required more employees to support the growth and serve the customers. The growing company increased its employees from ten or fifteen in 1920 to some one hundred employees in 1930, and to more than one hundred fifty employees by the time of its thirtieth anniversary in 1946.

Managers worked seven days a week in those days. But Murray felt strongly that they should have a day off. As the company grew, and as Murray assumed more responsibility, one of his well-intentioned changes involved giving managers a day off, even during the height of the company's busy summer season. But on their first day off, they all went to the beach and got such bad sunburns they couldn't return to work until two days later. So one day off turned into two. Murray said his father gave him hell for it. But he refused to go back to a seven-day work week. Even though the idea initially backfired, times were changing and the company had to evolve or they would otherwise lose qualified employees to the competition.

Over time it became clear that the workforce, and the manner in which employees viewed their roles, was

*Nathan and Ida, circa 1940-1950*
*Photo credit: Handwerker family collection*

constantly changing. In fact, there was even a worker's strike just before my father went off to war. Labor-management strife was becoming a major problem for business owners. My father told me that it became so bad that the workers actually slashed management's car tires, prompting Mayor Fiorello LaGuardia to intervene because of Nathan's high profile in Brooklyn at the time. Summer was coming and the mayor probably wanted peace in Coney Island, which started with peace at Nathan's Famous.

But growing pains were not just limited to issues between management and employees. Nathan's unique service method at the store eventually resulted in unexpected problems within the business. Because of the sheer volume of product sold, every type of food had its own counter and counterman to serve it. For example the customer would go up to one section of the counter to buy a frankfurter and then stand in another line if they wanted a different type of product.

Union leadership wanted each "counterman" to be responsible for serving one menu item only, with no cross job training. This would have required Nathan's to hire people for one position only, preventing them from doing anything other than the individual job for which they were trained. Nathan could quickly see the problem with that practice. If a worker quit, or called in sick, there was no cross-compatibility, and that particular job could go unfilled for the day. Thus, Nathan's stance was to hire more "managers" who would not be subject to the hiring and operating job description restrictions. Nathan thought he solved his problem. But the union was not happy with Nathan's approach and called a strike.

A meeting was arranged at LaGuardia's office, where Nathan, Murray, and the union heads began to negotiate the terms to settle the disruptive issues. There was no progress until my grandfather stood up and told the room full of people, "If we have to have all men work only one station, I will close the store down and everyone will lose their jobs—and I will turn the building into a carousel, because these horses don't eat or shit!" Everyone started laughing. That broke the ice and led to some open conversation. More importantly, that comment made the union understand Nathan's final position, and they ultimately reached agreement, knowing that he meant business.

Nathan had a knack for finding solutions to difficult problems, whether within his business or outside of it. Unfortunately, I wish it had been so easy to negotiate the strife simmering between family members in later years.

> **Frank Lesson:** *Always stand your ground. Understand the problem, your upside and the downside, and then determine the most acceptable solution. Don't just bend to the will of others.*

## Clashing Management Styles

The biggest business negotiation Nathan could not bring to an amicable solution was among himself, Murray, and Sol. With day to day business decisions always in question the brothers and Nathan could not agree on how to move forward with many issues. Ever heard the term "too many cooks in the kitchen"? Well, for Nathan's Famous, there were way too many managers with different agendas and leadership styles.

Murray insisted on opening a second location in the 1950s, when the Coney Island neighborhood began deteriorating and many baby boomers moved to the suburbs. Murray tried to convince his father to follow them and open a location closer to their homes. Nathan would have none of this talk of an additional location. Unlike his begrudging acquiescence to menu expansions, this time he put his foot down.

But Murray was hell-bent on giving his vision of growth a try. It probably caused enormous pain to my grandfather when Murray left Nathan's and bought himself a huge sit-down restaurant in Oceanside and renamed it Murray's Roadside Rest. It would prove to be a bumpy ride for father and son.

*Section 2*

# THRILL ON THE
# STEEPLECHASE

## 1950 – 1960's

*William in Nathan's arms looking at Kumquat tree
and tasting the fruit for the first time.*

## Chapter 3

# Murray's Venture Outside Coney Island

*D*uring the mid-1950s, Murray recognized that borough neighborhoods like Coney Island were in the early stages of a major transition. Amusement parks, which were at the center of the Coney Island experience, began to disappear. Many had burned down or were crumbling from disrepair. In 1944, almost half of the Luna Park amusement park (one block east of Nathan's) burned down. It did not reopen even with the end of the war in 1945, when the world was getting back to normal. Steeplechase (two blocks west of Nathan's) was the last of the three great amusement parks left standing. Fortunately, with the resurgence of Coney Island today, Luna Park has reopened better than ever! At that time many independent rides and penny arcade games dotted the Bowery. These rides and games would later provide me with many memories, including childhood birthday party experiences that I will never forget.

While Nathan's business was holding its own due to quality food and a low price structure, my father told me that our strategy of a lower price structure resulted in a lower profit margin for the menu. However, we enjoyed higher sales because the menu was accessible to a larger customer base, which therefore resulted in a greater bottom line profit.

Murray felt we could implement this operating philosophy elsewhere in the Metro New York area. He told me that it is imperative to grow and evolve. We could not stand still; we must move forward. Our Coney Island location was clearly the flagship of the organization and would always be what I refer to as "the Motherland," where it all began.

But times were changing. Coney Island and the rest of Brooklyn were welcoming home WWII veterans with open arms. Meanwhile, these men and women had one more significant role to play in our country's history: to create the Baby Boom Generation. The population was growing fast and families—including my parents—flocked from the city to the suburbs. Just before I was born in 1954, my family moved from Brooklyn to Lawrence, New York on Long Island. My family was just one example of young parents seeking a better quality of life for their children. Thus, it was only natural for my father to follow his dream of opening a second location in Oceanside on Long Island, so beachgoers wouldn't have to *schlepp* to Coney Island to savor the flavors of Nathan's red hots.

> **Frank Lesson:** *Be aware of trends in your industry as well as the area in which you operate so you can adjust the course, take advantage of new opportunities, or decide when it's time to cut your losses.*

## The Roadside Rest Is History—
## A New Nathan's Restaurant Opportunity

The Roadside Rest, a famous restaurant on Long Beach Road in Oceanside, had closed in 1955. Founded in the 1920s, at its height this once-hip institution sat as many as three thousand diners.

My mother and father would tell me stories about the big-band greats such as Benny Goodman, Lionel Hampton, Tommy Dorsey, and Eddy Duchin who

*Original Roadside Rest old postcard, circa 1937*

*Garden Terrace of Roadside Rest old postcard*
*Photo Credit for both pictures: Howard B. Levy and the*
*1960 Sailors Association Inc. www.1960sailors.net*

would play regularly on the Roadside Rest's stage. They would pack the house while guests danced late into the night. The restaurant was an entertainment destination for years!

The Roadside Rest had suffered during WWII, as many musicians and potential patrons were drafted and sent overseas. Gasoline was rationed at home, making it hard for the remaining folks to get to the restaurant. After the war, theaters and houses became air-conditioned, and more and more homes got televisions, supplanting hot dogs and crinkle fries with TV dinners in the comforts of their own living rooms. As a result, the restaurant gradually fell into disrepair, and by 1955 the debt-ridden bistro shuttered.

Murray recognized other trends that he believed spelled opportunity. Long Beach Road was the major thoroughfare to the beaches on the Atlantic Ocean. As smaller communities sprouted up across Long Island, Murray was certain he could breathe new life into the restaurant. Dorothy was right behind my father and his belief in this concept. When they spotted an opportunity in the form of the Roadside Rest, Murray and Dorothy felt this was their shot to show Nathan they were making the right decision. They would have loved to turn it into a second Nathan's location, however they couldn't make that happen without Nathan's blessing.

Murray & Dorothy still insisted on taking advantage of the growing suburbs and expanding the family business. So in 1956 they went forward without Nathan's consent, planning a grand reopening of the Roadside Rest under the new name of Murray's Roadside Rest. It was much like the original restaurant with a successful fast-food type operation, but it also had a sit-down dining room called the Old English Room, which ultimately resulted in the downfall of the operation.

**Frank Lesson:** *Opportunity does not always come in additional sales. Sometimes focusing on doing one thing well is the best plan for success.*

The big problem was that in addition to a steakhouse menu, the sit-down Old English Room offered fast food in an elegant setting, which just didn't make sense in combination. It had waiter and waitress service with white tablecloths on every table. The margin on each of the menus was probably too low to recoup the expenses of marketing two different restaurant concepts under one roof. There was also a mismatch of clientele between those who dined at the sit-down restaurant and those who patronized the fast food section.

Both my parents worked their hearts out trying to make Murray's Roadside Rest successful. But after three years, they just couldn't make it work. My parents

*Old English Room wooden carving hanging in*
*Murray's Roadside Rest dining room, circa 1950s*
*Photo credit: Handwerker Family collection*

had invested everything they had in the restaurant and were suddenly in jeopardy of losing all they owned.

During this dire situation, they had to make a decision: continue to try making the sit-down restaurant work while risking everything, or cut their losses and close the restaurant. While there were other options, such as selling the place to another restaurateur, it seemed they either needed to fish or cut bait, even though the most obvious and easy solution would be to try to talk Nathan into buying them out and converting the restaurant into a Nathan's Famous operation—as Murray initially hoped to do from day one.

According to another cousin (who heard it from his father), Murray called his Uncle Joe, to act as an intermediary between him and Nathan to get the deal done and recover from this misstep. My father started by inviting Joe to the restaurant to show him the operation. When Joe saw the town of Oceanside and surrounding local communities, he understood why Murray and Dorothy had been working so hard to make the restaurant a success. Joe recognized that the population on Long Island was growing and indeed represented a great opportunity for anyone with the foresight to take advantage of the situation. Joe was onboard and ready to pitch it to Nathan.

After the two had met, Joe went back to Nathan to tell him "the kid [Murray was thirty-seven] has a great location for a Nathan's restaurant." Even though Nathan was still recalcitrant about purchasing Murray's Roadside Rest, he wanted Murray back into the fold of Nathan's Famous. Joe's input and his desire to have Murray back helped convince Nathan to agree to open a second Nathan's location.

The irony of the situation was that it was only through Murray's impending failure that he received exactly what he hoped for from day one: a Nathan's Famous location on Long Island. Murray managed ultimately to receive his father's approval to buy the Long Island location partly by showing Nathan his commitment to the concept of expansion. He also demonstrated a strong work ethic and dedication to creating a lasting legacy.

I believe Nathan was also impressed by his son's willingness to assume all the risks in following his desire to make this dream come to life. After all, about forty-five years earlier, Nathan put up his own money and took all the risk to open his first food stand. There was no difference here; like father like son. It was Murray's determination that finally motivated Nathan to agree to purchase the restaurant and convert it to the Coney Island-named institution, Nathan's Famous.

*Nathan's, Oceanside, NY, circa 1960*
*Photo Credit: Nathan's Famous website*

In 1959, when Murray's Roadside Rest became the second Nathan's restaurant, it was renamed again to Nathan's Roadside Rest. A few years later it would lose its "Roadside Rest" identity and be known just as Nathan's.

After the opening, Nathan retreated back to his sanctuary in Coney Island. This was his general practice with any of the store openings, like the later ones that opened in Yonkers and Times Square. Oce the establishment was up and running for business, Nathan would rarely step foot in those restaurants again.

Regarding the Long Island location, Murray publicly stated that it was Nathan who insisted on buying him out. In one interview with Howard B. Levy and the 1960 Sailors Association Inc.[9], Murray said, "My father was very concerned that I would have less of an involvement with the Nathan's operation if I stayed involved with Oceanside, and he came to me and wanted to know if I was willing to merge it into the Nathan's organization. I knew what the potential was with Nathan's, but I wasn't 100 percent sure of the *long*-term [Murray stretched that word] advantage of being with Nathan's rather than being on my own. So we thought about it because my wife and I really went all out to put all our own personal investments into that operation. It was ours. The result was that Nathan's, of course, took it over with a long-term lease, and then I sold out everything."

I'm sure that my parents' decision to convert the restaurant was a very difficult one. But it was the right choice for everyone, because in the end, I believe that Murray belonged with Nathan and the company. This was also the first step to making Murray's grand dream of turning Nathan's into a chain come true.

> **Frank Lesson:** *Never give up on your dreams. Follow them, support them, and do all you can to obtain them.*

For the grand reopening on June 4, 1959, the local newspaper, *Newsday*, featured ads inviting the community to come for free hot dogs, drinks, and ice cream. It was a madhouse throughout the day and night. One 1960 high school graduate reminisces that he convinced his driver's ed. teacher to let their car full of student drivers pull up for the free food. He and some of his classmates returned after the school day for another round of free fare, and then brought their parents and siblings back for dinner![10]

Once Murray was back in the fold and operating under the Nathan's Famous banner, the huge building with picnic-style tables became the go-to destination year-round for families and students with empty stomachs. Whether returning home after a long day at the beach, or after high school football or basketball

---

9    Howard B. Levy and the 1960 Sailors Association Inc. www.1960sailors.net
10   Howard B. Levy and the 1960 Sailors Association Inc. www.1960sailors.net

games, or to hang out with friends and relatives, Nathan's became the destination for one and for all.

My parents used promotional events, including an eclectic range of entertainment like jazz music, singalongs, and square dancing, as well as weekend puppet shows for the children, to promote sales at the restaurant. There was a children's park with rides next door, called KiddieLand Park, which featured a carousel. A clown named Jazzbo took over the little amusement park and renamed it JazzboLand, operating it until 1965. This welcomed in droves of families, and after a long day at the park they were hungry and ready to eat at Nathan's.

Another event held at the restaurant was with the New York Giants football team. One or two members of the team would come down on Monday nights. I met Spider Lockhart (the starting defensive back for the Giants) there when I was a kid. He impressed me as a real humble guy who enjoyed talking to the crowd. He was great with the kids—including me. These weekly visits were a big deal.

In those days, the Giants' home games were blacked out from being viewed on TV in New York. People used to drive to Connecticut for home games and rent motel rooms to party in and watch the game on television. For the rest of us, we were lucky enough to have the experience of watching game films at the Oceanside Nathan's on Monday nights, while also listening to one of the Giants' players talk to us about the prior game.

Usually hundreds of people would come to enjoy these evenings to listen to the player and have a Q&A period, while eating Nathan's franks and other menu items. Every fan had a great time. The reality is that we had a varied customer base, all of whom enjoyed Nathan's fare. Our customers ranged from hungry families to high school seniors with their first cars to motorcycle clubs. The bikers would often sit all the way in the back of the restaurant. They tended to mind their own business. If we had any problems, it was always some guy trying to impress his girlfriend by attempting to take on a biker, rather than the other way around. The bikers were excellent customers—they had huge appetites and drank a lot of beer, and they rarely created a problem in the restaurant if they were left alone. I can still envision the line of twenty-five to fifty bikes all across

Long Beach Road. They did create some issues with the local residents riding through the streets at night.

In the later years management created a "Bike Night" for regular middle-aged guys who owned a motorcycle. They would ride in with their bikes to convene over a meal and have a beer while bonding over bike talk.

In the 1970s, Classic Car Night was another popular phenomenon. People with old cars would contact one another and agree to meet in the Nathan's Oceanside parking lot with their restored classic cars. The objective was simple: grab a bite to eat, enjoy a cold beer or three, and schmooze about their cars. Everyone had a great time reminiscing about the "good old days."

Nathan's was a gathering place for all generations, all ethnicities, all socio-economic backgrounds, and plenty of people with different interests. Nathan and Murray worked to create a welcoming environment for all. No matter the walk of life, they understood that the business should be comfortable, inviting, and put a smile on people's faces.

In 1966, and in concert with the fiftieth anniversary of the flagship Coney Island store, the Oceanside store expanded its menu to include charcoal-grilled meats. This decision was met with considerable fanfare, as the customers loved a hamburger or piece of chicken from the grill.

With decisions like these, the restaurant chugged along nicely. In 1976, while profits were still flowing at the Oceanside location, the forty-seven-year-old building itself became too much of a burden to run profitably. The sheer size of the building and the overall sales did not dictate maintaining the status quo.

It had to be torn down and rebuilt. A new, more modern, reduced-size structure was required to create a more profitable and well-run business. It took some time to build, but the operation became more manageable and profitable. And for the first time, the store changed its service methodology so that patrons could order most of their items in just one line. Despite its continuing popularity, the beloved Oceanside location closed in early 2015. However, a new Oceanside unit opened down the block in the spring of 2015, and the locals were happy they did!

The patrons cling to their nostalgic memories of the old store. The current management did a wonderful job in creating a unique décor reminiscent of the restaurant's storied past. I am one patron who certainly appreciated their effort. Although most of my childhood memories hail back to the Coney Island store, Oceanside still holds a special place in my heart. Even though my family lived closer to the Long Island beaches and the Oceanside restaurant, we preferred Coney Island because that's where all four of my grandparents lived, and that is where it all began.

## Coney Island Memories

Coney Island is the main source of my childhood memories. And for Nathan's Famous, it is truly the "Motherland." The memories I maintain from that location are endless. In the early 1960s, from the time I was between six and ten years old, we did not have air conditioning in our blue station wagon. So it felt like we were trapped in the car every trip to Brooklyn during the summer to visit my grandparents in Coney Island and Brighton Beach. It was like riding in a steam bath.

We would pile into the car and drive the same route to Coney Island, heading under the "El" train in Far Rockaway to Beach Channel Drive to the Marine Parkway Bridge to the Belt Parkway. We would go on our journey to Brooklyn from our home in Lawrence, Long Island. As we inched closer to the restaurant, I would begin to get excited to rush out of the car and start the day. I knew we were almost there as we passed the handball courts, which produced some of the best players in the world, the aquarium, and then the infamous Cyclone rollercoaster.

We drove into Coney Island with all the windows rolled down so we could feel the ocean breeze along Surf Avenue. We knew we had arrived when we heard the rumbling of the Cyclone's coaster cars—the world's fastest rollercoaster on wooden tracks. We'd hear the helpless screams of those daring people who chose to get the thrill of their lives on this monster of a ride. To this day I have never gone on the Cyclone, and I have no plans to do so.

Being a part of the Handwerker family, we were able to park in the small parking lot behind the Nathan's Famous restaurant. Once we exited the car, we enjoyed the competing smells of the ocean, freshly cut crinkle french fries frying, and hot dogs grilling. It felt like I was home again, comfortable with the surroundings and ready for fun! Mix in the sounds of screaming kids and adults on the rides, and the popping sounds of the shooting galleries, and we were all overcome with smiles, closing our eyes and knowing we had arrived at a familiar place.

These memories of Coney Island are forever imprinted in my memory. As I would stand outside the car waiting for my mom and brothers to get out, I would feel the heat of the sunbaked sidewalk through the soles of my sneakers. My high-top "Cons" felt like they were melting on the sidewalk on the hot summer days. As I walked through the small parking lot behind the restaurant, I was excited to turn the corner to see all the people hanging around the sidewalk outside our family's restaurant, waiting for friends or family who were in line for their food.

Once we arrived at the restaurant, another family perk was to be able to sit down inside a small dining room we called the "Green Room," because of the painted sea-foam green colored walls. It had eight to ten tables with waiter service. The entrance to the dining room, off Schweikerts Walk, was across from the corn stand and the bumper car ride exit. We didn't go into the dining room from the regular entrance, as we knew that Grandma, Grandpa, and my dad would be upset if we didn't say hello to them by first going through the back and into the kitchen.

When entering the kitchen, my mother, brothers, and I were greeted with smiles and hugs by some of the older, longtime employees. After we said our hellos, we stopped in on my father, grandfather, and grandmother, who would either be working in the kitchen or on the counter front line. They would all be bustling around, but never too busy to give us a hug before we began our day at Coney Island.

We were ready to order our lunch after we went into the dining room. Funny enough, and to the horror of my parents and grandparents, I actually hated frankfurters in my early years. I only wanted to eat the hamburgers and fries. This was sacrilegious, but what did I know about my legacy? I had no clue at that age that my grandfather had launched the most famous hot dog stand in New York. What did I know that his french fries also were considered the best in New

*Former dining room in Nathan's Coney Island*
*Photo credit Bill Mitchell photography*

York? All I knew was that I loved the hamburgers and fries, and that was good enough for me.

After lunch, we would visit with my mother's parents, Zoya and David Frankel, and then go to the beach with them. It was a production to gather everything we needed for the beach: blankets, a radio, drinks, and toys to keep a little kid like me busy for a few hours. It seemed like eternity to get to the beach and then walk on the burning sand from the Boardwalk to the water. Once your feet hit the sand, it seemed like the water was miles away. We would find an open spot in the sea of people where we could set up two or three blankets to sit on for my two older brothers, Ken and Steve, my mother, grandparents, and me.

God forbid we would step on another family's blanket! It's a miracle that I didn't get lost every time we went because of all the people on the beach. I loved the ocean and the sound of the waves against the beach. I can still remember trying to body surf (without the need of a board) on those days when there were sufficient waves to do so. It was a simple pleasure and something I always looked forward to doing. In fact, it's something I still enjoy to this day.

The Good Humor man would walk the beach all day with a white freezer box filled with ice cream bars, screaming, "Ice cream, who wants Good Humor Ice Cream?" Dressed in white shorts, a black belt, a white button-down shirt, and a white formal Navy hat, he would walk the steamy beach and bring a kid's dreams to life. It was so hot and the ice cream was so cold that we always had to have one before the end of the day. The ice cream man made a killing on those hot summer days.

While at the beach, I had a great time playing in the sand and the water. After a long day, the family would pack up the blankets and our leftovers, walking off the beach while full of sand and tired from swimming in the ocean. In the late afternoon, after the sun had beat down on the beach all day, we had to dance, hop, and run to the Boardwalk to avoid burning the soles of our feet. To avoid getting sand in our shoes, we didn't put them on until we reached the Boardwalk. It was worth the additional pain. We couldn't wait to get to the creaking wood planks of the Boardwalk; they were our safe haven from the "hot coals" of the beach, even though one of us would inevitably get a splinter from walking barefoot on the wooden boards.

We would go back to Zoya and David's apartment to rinse off, and then pack into the back of my mother's car for the dreaded ride home. My brothers and I would fight for a spot in the car's back storage area, as that was where we kept the blankets and pillows. Being the youngest, I usually lost and had to sweat it out in the backseat for the duration of the journey.

**Frank Lesson:** *Don't forget where your ride began. Good times will always put a smile on your face.*

## Steeplechase on My Ninth Birthday

In 1963 I was about to turn nine, and my mom asked me how I wanted to celebrate my birthday. My choices included bowling for the millionth time with my friends, followed by mediocre hamburgers and a cake; a double feature at the local theater with stale popcorn and boxed Good & Plenty or Sno-Caps; or a trip to Coney Island for lunch at Nathan's, plus carnival games and rides. Which birthday party do you think a bunch of nine-year-old kids would most prefer?

My mission was to convince my mom to herd as many of my friends as possible in the back of the station wagon for a day of pure fun in Coney Island. She was the best! In fact, she let me take four or five of my closest friends for the day.

Leading up to the party, I worried that the weather would not cooperate. For the entire week before my party, I remember not talking to my mom and dad about anything other than my anxiety regarding the weather. I actually prayed for a sunny day.

My grandfather Nathan and my dad would often opine, "Don't waste your energy worrying about something you have no control over." This insightful remark was intended to cover more than just birthday weather. But at age nine and facing my special day, I became quite the fan of the daily weather, intently listening to updates regarding Coney Island.

Luckily, the weather was perfect that Saturday. My friends came over early so we could hit the road and try to beat the traffic. And this time I had the upper hand on where I sat in the car during my birthday trip. No fights with my brothers! My friends got to choose who would have to sit in the backseat. In typical birthday boy fashion, there was plenty of room next to my mom in the front of the car.

The famous horse race at the Steeplechase amusement park was my favorite Coney Island ride of all time. When we reached the entrance, we were in awe of the size of the towering white arch with the colorful, smiling Tilyou face greeting us. However, we had to make an important choice before we entered: Do we go through the spinning giant barrel with air shooting up to blow up the dresses of the women, or walk around the side? Well, it wasn't much of a decision at all. We all walked through the spinning barrel. But of course my mom went around the side.

We quickly made our way to the exciting Steeplechase ride. Horses from a carousel were on a track eight abreast. At the beginning of the ride, riders would each climb onto their horse, and then be hoisted up like a rollercoaster, but with a climb less steep. The horses would wind around the building on a constant, slight decline so gravity could propel the riders during the "race."

Everyone would start at the same time, taking off like they were at a real horse race. At my party, and because we were young and small, the workers put two of us kids on one horse and clasped

*Vintage postcard of the Steeplechase Park Horse Race ride, Coney Island, NY, circa 1920s*

the leather strap around both of us. Still, we'd always lose since we were such lightweights. At the height of the ride, we were about twenty feet in the air with no safety net underneath. We'd have no choice but to hang on for dear life.

That year I shared a horse with Marc, one of my oldest friends and someone with whom I still remain in touch with today. On this amusement attraction, the more each rider would lean forward, the more the breaks on the horse would release. The horse would slow down when Marc and I both leaned back. But we obviously chose to lean forward. On the horse next to us, we noticed a hefty older guy with a hat. Based on sheer physics, we didn't stand a chance to win. But about three-quarters of the way around, and coming down the homestretch, trailing behind this guy, our luck changed when the wind picked up his hat.

As he leaned backward to try to catch it, his breaks came up, slowing him down. Marc and I leaned forward as far as we could on our wooden racehorse to gain momentum and hopefully win the race. Thanks to the wind, we were first to cross the finish line! That memory of Coney Island will thrill me until the day I die.

This probably was one of my first experiences with how just a little bit of luck and timing can create success. But it also taught me that life is not always fair. Winning and losing can sometimes be arbitrary, requiring no amount of skill, preparation, or hard work to obtain success. It can come and go with the wind. Of course, without all those elements, the odds are stacked against us. But even when we are at the bottom of the stack, luck can be on our side.

> **Frank Lesson:** *Make your own luck. But understand that no matter how hard you try, an unexpected gust of wind may always change your fate.*

At some point between rides, my friends and I took a break and headed for the Nathan's stand to stuff our faces with all the hot dogs, burgers, fries, and ice cream we could eat. We had to test ourselves: Could we keep the food down? Who was going to throw up first? Fifteen minutes later, we would argue about which ride we wanted to head to next.

"Boys, choose a couple of slow rides," my mom warned. We all responded with, "Let's go on the Tornado!" We all knew it was faster, and the turns and drops were steeper than the Thunderbolt coaster. Luckily, we survived the day with our food still intact. I remember that day as one of the most memorable birthday parties I ever had. I will always remember the annual Coney Island adventures throughout my early years. The twists and turns we experienced on my birthdays in Coney Island were out of pure joy. But in hindsight, they were not nearly as fast or steep as the twists and turns happening in my family and the business, such as Uncle Sol leaving to start Snacktime.

## Family Management Shakeup

When it came to the family business, I still remember hearing from both my mother and father about the Coney Island location. Murray, Sol, and Nathan would have their share of disagreements about management decisions. With company management, running a family-owned business adds another level of complication.

In the case of Nathan's, the brothers' individual management-style differences—along with Nathan and his first-generation business focus of family survival and success—became a problem for the three of them. It seemed that Murray and Sol were usually in disagreement about how to make decisions in general, and then how to set priorities for growing the company. It was always a struggle to get the two of them to agree on just about anything. Unfortunately, the company's decision-making process was strained by the three different opinions and management styles that Nathan, Murray, and Sol brought to the table. They all had the best of intentions but felt there were substantially different ways to reach the destination.

There were big changes occurring within the family business. While Murray was out of Sol's hair until he returned in 1959, Sol still had his own issues with Nathan. In 1963, Sol made his grand exit from Nathan's and opened his own restaurant, Snacktime, on 34th Street in Manhattan.

After Nathan's went public in 1968, the company had to disclose the financial arrangements it made with Sol. I found in our family records a Nathan's stock proxy from 1973 outlining the deal struck between my Uncle Sol and Nathan's. It also stated the financial relationships with other family members. When Sol opened Snacktime, Nathan's allowed his restaurant to advertise and sell Nathan's frankfurters and offered other financial support, like stock options and an annual salary.

This not only demonstrates that Sol left Nathan's with a deserved financial arrangement for all of his work, but it also illustrates that my grandfather and father wanted Sol to be successful by supporting his business with Nathan's franks. Even though Sol branched out to prove he could succeed on his own, the family bond still held true, as demonstrated by the company's payments to Sol. To my knowledge, no non-family-owned business would ever give their featured product to a competitor to advertise and sell without profiting from the sale of the product.

**Frank Lesson:** *Family matters. You may not always agree with their decisions, but never cease to offer them much-needed support.*

After his brother left, Murray enjoyed free rein and was named president of the company in 1968. The title came with many fiduciary duties. However, Sol was not completely out of the picture. He still owned shares of the company and part ownership of the family real estate portfolio. Murray had no major issues with Sol and the family real estate investments, as he deferred to Sol during negotiations that represented the family's interests. It was important that Murray did not represent the family at the same time as he was the company President. It would be a conflict of interest to represent both parties during any Coney Island lease negotiations.

Coney Island, Oceanside and Yonkers were the original three stores. I wonder how Sol viewed the company and its growth in the late 1950's and early 1960's.

## Questions I Wish I Could Ask

While writing this book, I felt it was incumbent to try to speak to my Uncle Sol to get his personal perspectives, candid memories, feelings, and thoughts about the company's history. Unfortunately, this never happened. In retrospect, I started writing this book too late.

My Aunt Minnie and Uncle Sol are both elderly. Minnie has declined on Sol's behalf to meet with me about my desire to learn more. I can only conjecture about what happened among Nathan and his two sons. I wish I could go back in time and ask Sol many questions, including:

1.  What are your earliest memories of Coney Island, Nathan, and Ida?
2.  What is your happiest memory about working in the company?
3.  What was your proudest contribution to the company?
4.  What issues triggered the most contention between family members in years past?
5.  On which issues did you side with Nathan and your brother?
6.  How would you describe the differences in management between you and other family members? How were disagreements on major issues generally defused and resolved?
7.  How did you feel about Murray's initial expansion plans—first with the menu and, later, with locations such as Oceanside, Yonkers, and Times Square? Did you want to try and expand?

8. After you left Nathan's, Dorothy and Murray told me they tried to get you to come back to the company on a several occasions. What are your recollections about that?

I am very disappointed that I cannot get answers to these questions and many others. I would have loved to hear his perspective of the family story to add to my thoughts and current beliefs to reach a more comprehensive understanding.

## Work: A Means to an End?

After Murray turned around the Oceanside restaurant once it was converted to Nathan's, he was ready for a new challenge. It wasn't that he was greedy, wanting or needing to make more money. Rather, it was about his dream of seeing Nathan's become a national restaurant chain. Maybe it was a result of his college experience and what he learned at University of Pennsylvania and New York University that spurred his desire to do more than solidify his family legacy in Coney Island. Murray saw the potential of the Nathan's brand name. There had to be more growth ahead as a result of what his parents had worked so hard to create.

But Nathan didn't see the need to grow beyond his humble beginnings in Coney Island. He would ask Murray: How many stores did the family need to open to feed the different families? How many cars could each of the family members drive? How many roofs did they have to have above them? You can only wear one pair of pants at a time. After all, they had survived two world wars and the Depression. What was the point of expanding the company and taking on so much risk?

Nathan was certain that the Coney Island store could stand on its own forever. More important, he knew that the Coney Island location could provide enough money so that the family would have a comfortable life. For Nathan, his company was simply a means to that end. He couldn't understand the value in jeopardizing it all with a costly expansion that could cut into profits and drain savings.

But that's not the way my father viewed it. He viewed the company as a launching pad to bigger and better things. Until his dying day, Murray always felt a strong loyalty and nostalgia for the Coney Island flagship restaurant. However, he also recognized that Nathan and Ida created a very unique and special brand. While he didn't know exactly how to implement his expansion plan, he did maintain an all-consuming desire to market the product nationally and internationally to the consuming public.

For all the trials and tribulations the family business experienced due to the differing opinions, leadership, and management styles, these various viewpoints and thoughts also pushed Nathan's to a higher level of success than Nathan could have ever reached on his own. With any family business, you are always fortunate to have a think-tank's worth of minds that will help to guide the direction of its success.

The decision to grow was based partly on the concept of how the work ethic unfolds in different generations and their respective economic strata. When my grandfather and his generation emigrated to the U.S., their work ethic reflected their yearning to improve their financial condition and prevent their families from suffering the same wretched conditions that they endured in the "old country." They built a business to survive, not to flourish in a way that could jeopardize a "Family" business focus. Nathan always viewed franks as a way not just to feed his customers, but also to feed his family.

These immigrants worked all their lives to ensure they had enough to live on to create a better way of life for their children, while instilling principles like hard work and resilience. They made certain their kids received a good education, while offering true job security with an opportunity to join the family business if they so desired, but not without a willingness to work hard and start from the bottom.

Nathan was one of the hardest working guys around. Until he was in his late fifties or so, he rarely took time off to enjoy life. But as he aged and the company grew, Nathan began spending more and more winter weeks in Florida.

Outside of work, fishing was the only distraction or hobby that I can recall my grandfather enjoying. For years he had a stuffed sailfish hanging over his office desk. I remember a picture of him standing beside a boat captain and a hanging fish that measured taller than Nathan himself. Both Nathan and Ida enjoyed fishing as you can see below. When I was a young child, I remember going fishing with him off his backyard dock in Florida. It wasn't often, but it is a memory I won't forget.

For second-generation Americans, hard work and an endless work ethic were more often a means to an end, not the end itself. Many second-generation Americans seemed to work just as hard as their parents did, but they also cherished their down time after a hard day's work and looked forward to eventually retiring to relieve themselves of the rat race and day-to-day work pressures, while enjoying the pursuit of new and old interests.

For as long as they maintained their careers, both of my parents worked extremely hard and loved what they did. At the Oceanside restaurant, they labored day and night, mostly to ensure that the substantial gamble they made

would be a success. They felt the added pressure of the family assets and savings on the line, as my father risked it all on his dream of opening a restaurant in the suburbs. However, unlike Nathan, they definitely wanted to enjoy the fruits of their labor and not let life pass them by. In fact, they traveled the world together whenever they had the chance.

These trips would replenish Murray's tank and restore his energy so he could invest it back into his dream of taking Nathan's national. His next venture on that path would be a third store, in the county of Westchester, New York, in the city of Yonkers, which eventually opened in 1965.

*Nathan and Ida's Catch of the Day, circa 1960s*
*Photo Credit: Handwerker Family collection*

Murray felt that we could take advantage of our brand recognition in the entire New York City area with a simple expansion strategy. One restaurant in each borough or surrounding county. Murray felt that the large sized facility that comprised a Nathan's restaurant operation could be very profitable if it was located on a main road in the central business district of a highly populated area. The residents of Westchester could now be able to enjoy the Nathan's Famous dining and entertainment experience. Central Avenue in Yonkers met all the criteria. But the restaurant would not happen without yet another wrestling match with his father.

These two approaches to maintaining a work/life balance have instilled two very different perspectives in my life. My own take is a bit of a blend between my grandfather's and father's approaches to work and leisure. I believe in giving it your all while you are at work. But unlike those that came before, I try to limit my work hours in an effort to maintain a balance and remain both physically and emotionally present for my family. Generally, I try to leave most stress at the office and unwind once home. I feel blessed that I have the ability to do that.

> **Frank Lesson:** *Prioritize your family above all else. Work hard to create balance in your schedule, finding time for the most important people in your life.*

My parents used to say that people must love the work they do to be happy. It didn't matter to them if my brothers and I were doctors or waiters at a restaurant. No matter what line of work we chose, it was essential to try our best. However, they instilled in us that whatever profession we undertook, we should ensure it provided for our family in a manner that fit our chosen lifestyle. They told us we could be successful with hard work and effort in any industry or company.

As parents, we want the best for our children. But all we can do is instill a strong work ethic and set a rock-solid example. Money is often an ancillary result of hard work and treating people right. My grandfather is a prime example of an individual who put family first and realized a comfortable living in the process.

## Yonkers: Store Number Three

On the fifth anniversary of the then successful Oceanside location, Murray replicated the formula and took over another beloved restaurant. In this case, the newest opportunity came in the form of the five-hundred-seat Adventurer's Inn, which had opened in 1955 on 2290 Central Park Avenue in Yonkers. For nostalgic purposes, Nathan's kept the Adventurer's Inn logo in the terrazzo stone tile floor at the entrance of the restaurant, as well as the big pinball and arcade game room and a mini amusement park adjacent to the restaurant.

One issue that started to become apparent in our restaurant concept was the service method, which was the same at all three locations; the customer had to stand in different lines to buy the food and drinks. This method was a common service method during the early years of fast food, but was very inconvenient for customers going from line to line for their total meal. Eventually a change was in store for all Nathan's operations.

In 1964, and just before purchasing the Adventurer's Inn, Nathan's sold more than 8 million hot dogs a year at its two locations, plus another 2 million pounds of crinkle french fries, about 102 tons of shrimp, half a million corned beef sandwiches, and 14 tons of frog's legs. The menu offered about 70 items. Additionally, Nathan's had a thriving catering business. The company was on a *roll* (pun intended), and Murray was more convinced than ever that he could open a Nathan's in each city across the country, not limiting the business to every borough of New York City or every county in the surrounding area.

One of main reasons my father liked the Adventurer's Inn was its menu diversification. It had a delicious bakery that was an institution in Yonkers. In fact, that bakery was so fantastic it attracted a breakfast club every morning. A number of retirees visited solely for the baked goods and the central location of the restaurant. From 7 a.m. to 9:30 a.m. every day, the "breakfast club" would take over ten tables and order boatloads of coffee and danishes.

My mouth still waters when I think of the baker's wonderful sticky buns. Each and every time I went to the Yonkers store, I'd bring home four of them. When you walked into the store the aroma of the fresh baked danishes, cookies, cakes and those famous sticky buns with nuts and honey drizzled on top was almost too much to resist! My wife, Amy, and our kids loved the sticky buns almost as much as the hot dogs and fries. We would unravel the buns, which were almost a foot long, and savor each bite by eating the buns inch by inch.

After several years the original baker had to retire because the constant early-morning hours became too hard for him as he aged. Sadly, no one else could do the job the way he did it. The bakery goods were never the same. Over time, we closed the bakery because of the lack of experienced bakers.

Unlike Coney Island and Oceanside, Yonkers is not a beach community destination. The Yonkers restaurant does not attract throngs of sun-drenched, hungry families on a regular basis. But Adventurer's Inn did have one advantage: it was part of a growing trend of roadside attractions. It was a place for families where everyone could leave with a full stomach, while the kids burnt off energy playing in the game room.

Yonkers attracted even more of a mixed clientele than Oceanside. Shoppers from the Bronx visited because of the variety of shops in the area. Nathan's became a favorite hot spot for everyone.

But like the Oceanside operation, the Yonkers location did not come without its fair share of problems. For one thing, Murray didn't realize how rough the neighborhood could be. Fights sporadically erupted in and around the restaurant, causing significant safety concerns and sometimes even police involvement. Above all else, the restaurant had to provide a safe and welcoming environment for families.

Additionally, Murray did not anticipate the rise of Burger King and McDonald's, which were just establishing footholds in the tri-state area and training fast food diners that they didn't have to wait in line for each item separately, as they still did at Nathan's. In fact, they could get it all faster and for less money. Customers could stand on a single line and order everything at once at our new competitors' fast food joints. Outside of the flagship location, the Coney Island experience was becoming outdated, especially as more and more competing fast food franchises, such as White Castle and Wetson's, continued to encroach on Nathan's turf during the late 1960s and early 1970s.

As a result, both the Oceanside and Yonkers stores adapted to standard practices in the industry to meet customer expectations. First and foremost, patrons no longer had to wait in separate lines for each food item. Additionally, we revised the menu to meet evolving expectations. However, in the face of it all, the one thing that would never change was Nathan's standards of quality and value.

> **Frank Lesson:** *Be prepared to change with the times. Make concessions, but always remain true to the guiding principles that got you where you are.*

Eventually the Yonkers facility needed a facelift. In the early 1980s, we renovated the store to implement the standard fast food industry service methodology. Then, in 2013, the company tore it down and built a new, smaller unit that was a traditionally designed fast food restaurant operation which included some historical funky photos and murals of some old Coney Island scenes. The decision to rebuild had nothing to do with the success of the store. In fact, since reopening, it is as successful as the original restaurant with fewer operational issues. Throughout it all, the Yonkers restaurant has been quite profitable, but will always pale in comparison to the thriving Coney Island operation.

The first two expansions outside Coney Island were nothing compared to the sweat, tears, and exuberance Murray would face when he went for the brass ring: an initial public offering (IPO). In 1968, the company decided to offer the public a chance to own a piece of Coney Island history. The goal was to raise $2.4 million in capital to open a fourth location in the heart of Manhattan—Times Square—as well as to initiate ambitious franchising and licensing programs. But not every decision Murray made unfolded as he had dreamed.

> **Frank Lesson:** *Dream big. But maintain a willingness to assess and evaluate your dreams and constantly alter them to meet your needs.*

## Chapter 4

# Nathan's in the Public Eye

*A*s you can imagine, it was a watershed event for the company and the family when, in 1968, Nathan's went from a closely held family business to a publicly owned company. Murray became president that year while Nathan remained at the helm as acting CEO. With the proceeds of the public offering, Murray took the company by storm with several bold, concurrent expansion programs. Any one of these new efforts would have taxed the depth of Murray's management experience. That he attempted to dive into them all at once was amazing. And those encompassed just part of his responsibilities.

For the first time, Nathan's had to deal with outside shareholders, a board of directors, and government regulatory agencies. All of these new jobs could have easily been a recipe for disaster. But Murray maintained the self-confidence to overcome many unexpected issues that arose, while unbelievably managing it all.

## In the Public Arena

However, Nathan, who was seventy-five years old at the time, wanted little to do with the IPO or the resulting expansions. While he understood there was a large financial benefit by going public, his main concern was that it might put the Coney Island store at risk of being sold. He was also concerned that the family business was not so family-oriented anymore. That was such a huge concern for Nathan that he insisted on negotiating the right for the family to retain three twenty-year leases on the Coney Island restaurant property, which the family would own independently of the publicly held company. It was decisions like this that maintained the true foundation of the company, even when Nathan was no longer the only member of the board.

Nathan said if it were his decision he would use the money from the IPO to buy all the property he could in Coney Island, in an attempt to own the entire island eventually. But of course the company had other ideas for the growth of the business, and marketed such to the public. The goal behind the IPO was to expand on a national basis. Certainly Nathan could have used his portion of the proceeds to purchase property, but as I stated previously, Ida wouldn't hear any of that.

Despite Nathan's reservations about going public, I can picture him having to suit up and take the train to Manhattan, suffer through countless meetings and deliberations, and sign stacks of legal papers. That would have been punishment enough. However, he knew there was light at the end of the tunnel, as once the ink dried and he received his share of the money, I imagine him returning to Coney Island to put back on his Nathan's uniform, consisting of a short-sleeve white shirt and black slacks, and get back to work at the store in any capacity necessary.

In any event, it is no wonder more than one hundred brokerage firms bid for the rights to take our company public. At the time, fast food companies were hot. McDonald's had gone public in 1965, with Kentucky Fried Chicken doing the same the year after. Flurries of deals were inked the following decade, such as Pizza Hut in 1972 and Wendy's in 1976. During the same period, major corporations were acquiring fast food joints like they were going out of style. For instance, in 1967, the Pillsbury Dough Boy gobbled up Burger King's Whopper.

Through Nathan's lead underwriter, Michael G. Kletz & Co., the over-the-counter offering of 300,000 shares, priced at $8 a share, raised $2.4 million. Investors scarfed up the Class A shares (NASDAQ symbol NATH) with relish.

Day one, the stock quickly doubled to approximately $16 and closed at $14—75 percent higher than the initial offering price. By 1971, the shares frothed up to $42 per share, only to plummet a decade later to $1 per share when the company encountered severe problems.

The company wasted no time putting the funds to use. The main purpose of going public, in addition to opening additional company-owned locations, was to develop a network of franchises and to begin licensing packaged Nathan's branded foods. Nathan's used the IPO proceeds and other capital to obtain licenses to operate restaurants and fast food facilities in a museum, in a metropolitan ice skating rink, and in a convention hall in Brooklyn. It also made alterations and equipped restaurants located in Atlantic City and Greenwich Village, as well as completing its plans for the Times Square restaurant. Since it was the crown jewel of real estate in New York City, let's first look at the Times Square operation and the tremendous challenges encountered by each of the additional locations.

## Times Square: Hitting the Big Time

Murray was hungry to develop a presence in Manhattan, the biggest outpost of New York. His first choice was not just some out-of-the-way side street, but Times Square, the mecca of the most central, glitzy tourist destinations. In terms of exposure to the world, this was the place to be and was viewed as a steppingstone to rolling out restaurants both nationally and later internationally. Murray found a perfect spot for this work of art, the former Toffenetti's on the corner of 43rd Street and Broadway. With 28,500 square feet, the two-story location was one of the city's largest restaurants. Since its opening in 1940, Toffenetti's had become beloved, specializing in traditional American fare. It seated 1,000 diners—mostly tourists and theatergoers—and served more than 3,000 meals a day. The ground floor was the main room, and an escalator led down to a lower-level seating area.

Before the construction commenced, I remember visiting the location and seeing the shell of Toffenetti's that remained. When I walked through the main door, I recall seeing a huge display of Idaho potatoes as part of the décor. Once the location was transformed into Nathan's, I remember going to the upstairs office. I was about fifteen or sixteen years old, and I was overwhelmed to see the ornate bathroom located inside the office, which was like something out of a French palace. The upstairs space looked to me like a fancy law office.

While my father left the renovation decisions to two men who were eventually fired for the manner in which they handled the project, he likely approved the plans for the extravagant offices at the time. I can imagine him listening and believing the pitch that the company needed to impress potential future investors. To me it should have been the opposite way, the corporate headquarters should have been stark to keep management on the floor, not upstairs, and to convince investors the company would not frivolously spend its hard-earned money.

But my father had faith in his managers and let them do their job without putting his foot down. There was so much going on at the same time, including the company going public, the beginning of the franchise initiative, constructing the Times Square and Greenwich Village stores, developing a licensing business,

*Nathan's Famous Times Square, summer of 1970*
*Photo Credit: Bill Mitchell Photography*

and hiring scores of new people, that it would have been challenging for Murray to manage it all.

My grandfather was not happy about moving the office to Manhattan. He refused to move his own office and kept his desk, chair, and mementos where they had always been: on the second floor of the Coney Island flagship store.[11] After having accepted the previous two expansions in Oceanside and Yonkers, Nathan was not terribly upset about the newest expansion. He realized that the horse was already out of the barn.

While he was not exactly enthusiastic, I think he understood the objectives and went along with the journey. And he had to have been proud. After all, he and his son were both entrepreneurs. They went out and grabbed opportunities. If it didn't work, so be it. Regardless, it had to have been great for him to expand the business alongside his son.

Nathan understood Murray's expansion concept through the addition of the Big Apple location. It would provide huge exposure that could enable the business to work toward achieving brand recognition around the world. Nathan's Times Square (see photos) featured a glitzy, glowing neon Nathan's sign right on the corner of 43rd and Broadway. It was impossible to miss. Every New Year's Eve, the various TV stations would pan their cameras on it around midnight. In addition to the free television advertising, millions of people visited Times Square each year, and they would all see the sign for the restaurant that served the most delicious franks in the world.

While my father's original intent was to keep Nathan's headquarters at the Times Square location, they ultimately closed the upstairs offices in the restaurant. That glitzy space became a distraction for many of the employees. So the company initially moved the offices from 1401 to 1501 Broadway, and finally to 1515 Broadway, where the headquarters remained until the company was sold.

The 1515 office was actually a much nicer space, with huge plate-glass windows overlooking the Hudson River. But I remember hearing the whole building creak when the wind blew. During some of the more severe storms,

---

11    And there they remained, in fact, until Hurricane Sandy in October 2012, when the entire Coney Island store needed to be closed for the first time in its history and the store was renovated and reopened in April 2013.

I honestly felt the building sway and it scared the crap out of me. One of the intents of the office was to impress potential franchisees, and it did that quite well, without being nearly as ostentatious as the previous Times Square office.

Even with its great exposure, the Times Square location became a huge problem. Costs spun way out of control. It chugged along for many years, although it didn't always cover the location's huge and sometimes unnecessary expenses—such as the downstairs "Backroom" restaurant where the public and

*A normal Times Square lunch crowd, fall 1970*
*Photo Credit: Bill Mitchell Photography*

our own executives would bypass our normal front lines and dine. It wasn't exactly posh, but it was nicer than sitting at the Formica tables in iron-backed chairs. The main level dining room seating was intended to provide comfort to customers for an average fast food meal. The Backroom dining room allowed for more casual and leisurely dining with waiter/waitress service and the ability to stay as long as you desired.

While my father disapproved of the executives having lunch in the Backroom, he continued to let it happen, and it stuck in his craw. He told me that he would have expected us (including me) to stand in line at the store and experience what the customer does every day, without being told to do so. He reiterated his belief in the importance of customer satisfaction and for us to ensure firsthand that our service and products met their needs every day. My grandfather taught Murray, and Murray taught me that the customer's experience was what made us successful. He didn't have to say anything to me after that talk. After the conversation, I would often stand in the lines to test the service experience. As members of the family business, we all carried enormous responsibility to ensure that we did the best we could.

The Backroom at Times Square eventually closed, as did the entire downstairs part of the restaurant, leaving just the main level open for customers. That may have been exactly what the store needed. Maybe it became profitable at that point because of the reduced labor and reduced expenses of running two restaurants within one. But at the end of the day, we were locked into the lease. As long as we had to be there, our objective was to reduce the loss as much as we could. In business, you have to know when to cut your losses. We could still generate enormous profit through our other stores, so it was a matter of controlling the damage caused by our Times Square location.

In the end, the Times Square store became too much of a burden. Rent structures were outrageous for the massive store. Not that the Times Square store didn't generate huge sales, but at the time it was producing minimal profits. In 1990, we lost our lease due to eminent domain laws to make way for the first of four new office towers that were to house the new NASDAQ headquarters. I believe the public Urban Development Corporation bought out the lease in 1990 for about $1 million—a nice number in those days—which offset many of the sustained losses. At that point Nathan's moved its headquarters again, this time to Westbury, New York.

## New Stores, Bad Locations

In addition to the Times Square location, the company used some of the proceeds from the IPO to build another Nathan's in Greenwich Village in 1970, at the corner of Sixth Avenue and 8th Street, bringing the tally of company-owned stores to five. But while Murray's expansion was just gearing up, the Greenwich Village store created tremendous backlash. The community took a strong posture against Nathan's from day one, saying drug dealers and prostitutes were hanging out there and would often harass customers.

A long, drawn-out struggle with the community board ensued. A *New York Times*[12] article about the hoopla quoted Murray: "The community was not happy with us and we were not happy with them. They said it attracted the wrong people and I couldn't convince them that it wasn't Nathan's fault." In the end, the community won. In 1978 it edged out Nathan's from Greenwich Village. I chalk it up as a loss, but not nearly of the magnitude of Times Square.

> **Frank Lesson:** *You can't win 'em all. Do your best to play to your strengths and remain focused on your ultimate goals.*

Wall Street analysts at the time who covered the fast food industry were skeptical of the company's overall expansion plans. One commented that the plan was "impossible," saying "New York is their whole ballgame." Although the company had a rocky road ahead, the skeptics were proved wrong, at least in the long term.

Next on the expansion agenda was franchising.

## Foray into Franchising

The IPO prospectus indicated that "the company may use a substantial portion of the proceeds from its sale of shares for the initiation and development of

---

12  "Nathan's Hunt for an Upturn," *New York Times*, Sept. 19, 1981 http://www.nytimes.com/1981/09/19/business/nathan-s-hunt-for-an-upturn.html?pagewanted=all

a franchise department and the production and distribution to certain retail outlets of packaged foods under the 'Nathan's Famous' trade name."

The prospectus explained that the company "has made limited investigations of the feasibility of both operations and will not undertake either or both of these ventures until the results of further investigation indicate the desirability. Furthermore, the company has no experience in such operations and no assurance can be given that either or both, if undertaken, will prove profitable."

The prospectus also predicted losses during the initial years of these ventures (as is most often the case with startup projects), if the company were to embark upon either of them. Nathan's did undertake both ventures: the franchising and licensing of packaged hot dogs. And, as the prospectus predicted, initial financial results were disappointing.

Nathan's was in competition with all the other fast food restaurants around, both chains and those individually owned. At the time, many startup chain organizations were encroaching on the New York market and beyond. These chains were only ten to fifteen years old, while, in 1966, Nathan's had just celebrated its fiftieth anniversary. Murray was convinced that Nathan's could spread its longstanding reputation, quality product line, and service model throughout the country with its company-owned locations and through the infrastructure of franchising.

He felt that going public validated the company as a viable business. That made him more determined than ever to take Nathan's to the next level, if for no other reason than to support the decision to expand and go public. He believed that a successful business with the potential to scale up its model needs to grow or it will die. He was well aware of the hot trend in the late 1960s for fast food restaurants to franchise. McDonald's was well known in the late 1950s, mostly in and around the Chicago area, while Burger King was extremely strong in Florida. But neither had entered the New York market until the late 1960s. Because Nathan's had an early lead, my father was eager to try and make a go of franchising in the tri-state area.

Nathan's restaurant concept was built on the service premise that propelled the first three successful stores and attracted huge crowds. Murray wanted to replicate that service concept with the new franchises. At first we encountered mixed results. The first two franchises were in Hicksville and Staten Island, New York. Until we lost the lease some twenty years later when the landlord wanted a more upscale restaurant concept, the Hicksville location flourished. But the Staten Island franchise was not so successful. The company ended up buying it back, operated it for a while, and then, after it didn't work, decided to close it. We became awfully good at cutting our losses. When expansion didn't work, we strived to determine exactly why and improve the situation. If we could not improve it, we put it to rest.

In the early 1970s, Jack Skirball became a franchisee of Nathan's in the Los Angeles area. That didn't work out either. The ex-New Yorkers there loved the food, but most people on the West Coast did not know the Nathan's brand, and the "single-line" service methodology simply didn't catch on there.

By then, McDonald's and Burger King were growing. As I explained in the previous chapter, the fact that our customers had to stand in one line to buy a hot dog and go to a different counter to buy a drink worked for a while. But when McDonald's, Burger King, and other competitors came barreling in, diners realized they could stand in one spot to get all their food at once. Simply put, it became more convenient and less time consuming. So our big monstrous stores no longer seemed like a positive experience. The food was great, but the Coney Island experience, which still worked at the Coney Island, Oceanside, and Yonkers stores, was not welcomed in other parts of suburbia.

The sparkle of the Nathan's experience started to wear off. Because our menu was so large, logistics precluded us from copying our competitors' "one line for all food and drinks" model. Something had to give! The world was advancing while our service methodology lagged behind.

But our growth didn't consist solely of uphill battles. We did develop several successful mall locations. Mall stores tended to be very successful because they attracted plenty of captive-market customers. The one at Kings Plaza (which still retained the old service methodology at the time) is still there today, but with an industry standard single-service line. Our Paramus Park restaurant, located in the first mall to have a food court, offered the single-line service, and also remains open today. That our relatively small company became part of the earliest evolution of malls, alongside McDonald's and other national fast food chains, is a testament to the viability of Nathan's concept.

As with all his expansion efforts, Murray took his shot, working hard to expand the Nathan's brand. But despite these and a few other successful franchises, Nathan's halted the practice of signing on new franchises for a while. As the company experienced ups and downs with different stores opening and closing, Murray managed to retain its overall vitality throughout these years while maintaining profitability. That is, until our next major move, the Wetson's acquisition, which wiped out all our progress.

## Wetson's Acquisition

My father pursued the third leg of his expansion efforts by traversing the acquisition trail. He looked to purchase the publically traded but now bankrupt Wetson's chain of fast food outlets. Carl and Herbert Wetanson founded the company. Our plan was to transform them into Nathan's restaurants. In 1975, after shareholders of Wetson's and Nathan's Famous approved the merger, Nathan's eliminated many of the locations because they were unsuitable for conversion into modern fast food restaurants.

Nathan's Famous hired many of the Wetson's staff to help with the transition as well as for the need of additional management of the stores. From 1976 until I left the company in 1996, I worked with Wayne Norbitz, and for a shorter period with his father, Harold. Both Wayne and Harold, from Wetson's, joined Nathan's as executives. I learned a lot from both of them. Harold taught me many things about the art of contract negotiations. I worked with Wayne in all aspects of the operations.

During my many conversations with Harold Norbitz he told me the Wetansons had intended to flood the tri-state area with Wetson's, no matter what the location. Many of their over seventy restaurants had failed or were failing because they over-expanded, and did so in less than prime locations. But they did have a major presence. Harold said that McDonald's approached Wetson's before it came to the East Coast and offered the Wetansons the McDonald's franchise rights for New York, New Jersey, and Connecticut, as well as shares of McDonald's stock. The Wetansons turned them down. They told the McDonald's folks, "Why should we go with McDonald's when we have been here for years and have an established reputation?" They obviously made a bad decision and overestimated their company's strength in the face of the incoming powerhouse of McDonald's.

Like the Times Square location and the franchising program, the Wetson's acquisition did not go exactly as planned. In fact, this deal almost brought the company to its knees.

**Frank Lesson:** *You are always one wrong move away from catastrophe. Consider your options carefully and remain calculated in the decisions you make.*

## Personal Effects

Despite all of our stuttering expansion efforts and the stress it created (especially for my father), going public proved to be pivotal to the company's growth and success. It did take some time for the company to find the right balance, and for the economy to recover from a three-year recession. The IPO also provided some significant benefits to Nathan and his three children.

For the family, the public offering was an opportunity for the stockholders (Nathan and Ida, Leah, Sol, and Murray) to diversify their individual holdings so they could make other investments while retaining control over Nathan's Famous. The Handwerker family members held onto a majority stake of the Class A stock while my father retained all of the Class B voting shares. If he were to leave or sell the company, or even die, those shares would then be sold back to the company and retired.

However, there was a downside to taking the company public. While the capital enabled my father to realize his dream of expanding Nathan's, it also came with huge (and sometimes unexpected) pressures. One of the largest disadvantages of public ownership is answering to the stockholders. While the family maintained control, we still went through the filings and answered to our shareholders. The new multifaceted and multilayered business was not nearly as straightforward as operating a single location in Coney Island, which wasn't all that easy to begin with! I remember my father shaking his head as he came home every night. On certain evenings, he was so noticeably aggravated that my mother would hand him a drink—three fingers of Jack Daniels—just to take the edge off of an especially crazy day.

During these exciting but tumultuous times, and now that I was old enough to get working papers, I jumped at the opportunity to work in the family business. I was never deterred by the stress my father experienced. During the summers, I went to work, as did some of my friends, while others traveled on teen tours. At the crack of dawn, another employee of the business picked me up and together we headed to work in Coney Island. I started in Coney Island versus Oceanside because I was able to get transportation by an employee who lived near us. He would pick me up on his way to work and drop me off at the end of the day. I am thankful that I had this experience of working at Coney Island, knowing that I would be with my dad and grandfather at the same time.

When we arrived in Coney Island we would park in a nearby lot under the "El." As we walked from the parking lot to the store, I could tell how busy the store had been the night before by the amount of garbage overflowing onto the streets: the pavement was often scattered with plates, Nathan's drinking cups, corn cobs, clam shells, and all the other remnants of the customers' enjoyment of Nathan's Famous food offerings.

Every day during my first week on the job I saw a homeless person sleeping next to the empty beer kegs stacked outside the kitchen doors. I didn't know what to do the first time I saw him, so I told the general manager (GM). He told me that his name was John and he sometimes worked at the bar across the street sweeping floors to earn enough money for booze. The GM told me that every now and again, he would give John a cup of coffee and a frank. He further indicated that John was harmless. I also learned from him that sometimes Nathan would feed the homeless and that he learned it was a good thing to help those in need.

Unfortunately, later that summer, after not seeing John for a week or so, I asked the GM if he knew where he was. He told me that John died, and I was upset. It was probably one of the first times I experienced an unexpected death of someone I knew. While he was not a family member or even a friend, I still felt a sense of loss when I found out he passed away.

I learned from my grandparents, parents, and now our employees that helping people is an integral part of life. To this day, I take pride in the notion that Nathan and his little hot dog stand always did what it could to give back to the community and care for those that couldn't support themselves who were both inside the business and/or in the local area. In that tradition, when I worked as a general manager, I took the opportunity to help a manager with a loan. The individual needed money to have a medical procedure and he couldn't afford to have the procedure done. It makes for a happier work environment when the employees know the boss does take care of their own. I learned this from the very first year working at Coney Island and from my parents throughout my years growing up in our house.

My father put me to work on the front service counter to start my career at Nathan's. I arrived to work at seven in the morning and set up the drinks, grills, steam tables, deli, seafood, and fry stations. I had to stock paper goods such as plates, cups, and napkins and specific items for each station, which included topping off the orange, grape, and pineapple drink dispensers while bringing out coffee packages and teabags for the drink stations.

As simple as my job seemed during that first summer, I knew it was important to do it well since there would be little time once the crowds descended from morning into the lunchtime crunch. After ensuring all was in good order, the GM needed me to be on the front counter for the usual lunch crowd, which began around 11:30 a.m.

I could sometimes take lunch after the rush, and I walked around to go "people watching," one of my favorite activities. I enjoyed taking that break and strolling down Schweikerts Walk and the Bowery while looking at the people enjoying themselves on a sunny day. But it only lasted a few minutes before I realized I had to get back to the reality of serving many of those same people.

We spoke a pretty unique language within the counter. We had some unusual terms in the business that we would shout out to place the orders. Some of these terms were in the form of numbers, such as "93" and "86." When we thought there was some trouble outside with customers, we would yell "93," which meant "Call the police!" When we were given a potentially counterfeit five-, ten-, or twenty-dollar bill, we'd yell "check out 86," which meant "We may have a bad bill or situation that requires a manager's attention, so please come to the station."

Some funnier work verbiage was the phrase "check out the ice on the counter," which meant that a good-looking girl was walking by and all the guys should take a look up front. Of course, most of the guys would react at the same time. This was a great way for us to break the frenetic pace and the constant demand of dealing with the hungry crowds.

When the crowds were ascending from the subway and bus station to go to the beach for the day, or going back to the trains and buses when leaving, we would yell to one another certain phrases. Unfortunately, during one of the summer days, it began to rain around 3 p.m., well before 6 p.m. when people would normally begin to leave the beach. The managers were going around the counter yelling "they're coming off, they're coming off!" I didn't know what was about to happen the first time I heard that, but I did brace myself for something special, which I still remember to this day.

Shortly after hearing that phrase, people crashed into the front counter area ordering fries and everything else on our menu, for what seemed like an eternity. The lines were more than ten deep with people who were jockeying in position to get to the counter and give us their orders. I never picked up my head except to make change for the next hour and a half. I would yell out "how many?" and the customers would yell back "two orders" or "three orders." I would then shovel fries into a number-three bag (the smallest bag we carried), hand the orders to the customers, take the bill, and make change in just under a minute.

It was exciting, tiring, and satisfying to find that we met the challenge and had the crowd under control. After days like that, I still remember coming home, jumping in and out of the shower, and then falling on my bed totally wiped out. I felt great!

I earned about one dollar an hour during my first full summer at Nathan's. In fact, during that summer I saved a few hundred bucks. After earning $1,300 during the next summer, I bought myself a stereo system at a local store named Newmark & Lewis.

**Frank Lesson:** *Reward yourself for your hard work. Reap the benefits of what you sow.*

On weekends during my high school junior and senior years, I was able to drive myself to work at the Oceanside store. As a senior I experienced working under the conditions of a union strike. My brothers Steve, Ken and I all did our parts to help out. Steve had been working in the business from the mid-nineteen sixties. During the strike he was in Coney Island working with management to help with the operations in various capacities. He also was fortunate to learn from Nathan and Murray when he was able to sit at the negotiating table with the union. I was enlisted to help out between the Times Square and Oceanside restaurants when they needed backup. Ken and I went into the city and worked in various positions as directed by the manager of the restaurant. There were a few employees that thankfully did cross the picket line and came to work that day. The kitchen staff was still short-handed. One of our first jobs for the day was to unload a truck with two hundred 50 lb. bags of potatoes. This was not an easy job even under normal circumstances, needless to say working under strike conditions made it much more interesting for us!

The whole experience was very nerve racking and I did feel the pressure of the situation. Outside of the store at the corner of 43rd and Broadway, there were some striking workers screaming and holding picket signs. When we were piling the bags on the flatbed hand truck I noticed that the workers were looking at us and a few screamed at us calling out "SCABS!" We just went on working. As this was going on I was thinking that maybe these guys would start a fight with us, but fortunately nothing happened. However, we did have our own problems with the potatoes!

Just when we finished loading the last hand truck full of 50 bags of potatoes, the cart turned over in the middle of 43rd street. The strikers were laughing at us while we were chasing potatoes rolling on the street and sidewalk from the broken bags. We completed picking up the potatoes and were both exhausted as well as embarrassed. We did what we had to do and felt good about helping out in a stressful time for my dad and all management.

On another weekend during the strike I offered a couple of my friends the opportunity to join me to go to work at Oceanside. We needed the additional staff and I thought that they would enjoy the experience. Randy and Jan joined me and they were posted at the drink and french fries stations. I was working at the hamburger station next door to them and I watched as they served the customers hour after hour. After that weekend I am sure both Randy and Jan had a new appreciation for the employees that work in the fast food industry. They told me that when they left for home they were sticky from the drinks and smelled like french fries! They were very hot, worn out, and had definitely earned every penny they made that weekend! I was really happy that they were able to help us out during a rough time.

Even though the strike occurred, I developed a great working relationship with both the line staff and the managers. In the late 60s and early 70s, we maintained a highly successful catering department that supplied food for large and small affairs. From deli platter packages to a full roasted turkey with all the trimmings, as well as many other hot entrees, we provided plenty of options for all kinds of exciting events.

I worked to make a few extra dollars and help out over the Thanksgiving holiday during my senior year. I remember we had more than 130 orders to prepare for both delivery and pick up. When you want to make everything as fresh as possible, that's a lot of orders! The staff roasted turkeys, top round roast beefs, fresh briskets, and boiled corned beefs all Wednesday afternoon and evening. I was scheduled to work at 4:30 a.m. on Thanksgiving Day and until all the orders were filled and out of the restaurant. I remember I was preparing meat platters and side dishes for hours. The platters had to be packed and affixed with labels to ensure the customers received their exact orders without fail.

We all worked extremely hard and had a great time in the process. While we worked more than twelve hours straight and were exhausted, we still planned to come in at 6:00 on Friday morning and get the kitchen back in order for the weekend. The manager and a couple of other employees decided to pull a prank on me that I have never forgotten.

These three "Pineapples" (a term of endearment we often used to refer to our peers) asked me to go into the warehouse and bring back a case of paper goods. I was running on fumes from my long Thanksgiving Day at Nathan's. At the time, I could hardly focus on anything. So I walked into the warehouse and the lights were partially off. The case of goods I needed was in the back area where there was just one small light on. When I turned the corner around a bunch of boxes that were stacked high, I saw what looked like a man's body in a Nathan's uniform with a knife sticking out of his chest and blood running down his clothes. I ran out of the room screaming my head off, only to find these three guys in the kitchen laughing hysterically! The sons of bitches scared the crap out of me!

> **Frank Lesson:** *Create a work environment that is enjoyable for all. It is possible to work hard and also have fun.*

We always found humor on the job. But it never took the place of our continuous hard work ethic and desire to provide people with the highest quality product and the best experience around. For example, one Sunday afternoon one of the regular clam men called in sick and the store was short staffed for the mid-afternoon shift. The manager asked me to cover for an hour or so until the nightshift came in around 6 p.m. I took my position at the clam sink with my own clam knife. The Sunday dinner crowd always came early. The whole time I was at the sink, we were constantly busy with customers until I left for the night.

For just over an hour, I shucked clams and was relieved when the nightshift arrived. I had a newfound respect for the regular clam men. My hands felt like blocks of ice. I could hardly feel the blood running through my fingers. I had to run my hands under warm water to attempt to thaw them out. But it was that all-in team attitude that made Nathan's so special. We were always willing to do what it took to get the job done, even if it wasn't a regular day in the office.

I always felt that I was part of the crew and would do the job no matter what was asked of me. I worked hard and learned a lot about the business from the bottom up. I got to know a lot of the employees, earned their respect, and developed a bit of confidence in my abilities and understanding of how the business actually operated. I enjoyed the pride of my father and grandfather while they watched as I worked hard and fulfilled the legacy they had created and were passing on to me.

I cherished opportunities to learn more about the company while dreaming of the day I could finish college and enter the family business on a full-time basis. However, that dream of working full-time alongside my father and grandfather never occurred, as Nathan Handwerker, the founder of Nathan's Famous, retired in 1971, just one year before I graduated high school.

In hindsight, we all came to learn that Nathan and Ida did not retire willingly. My father wanted both Nathan and Ida to enjoy life outside of work. He and my mother tried their best to entice them to take the time for themselves and relax. There were no motives behind my father's actions other than to give Nathan and Ida the opportunity to develop other interests and passions besides working behind the counter at Nathan's.

> **Frank Lesson:** *Don't let your work define who you are. Make time for the rest of your life.*

In my cousin David's interview with my grandfather, Nathan said, "I would be happy just to sweep the sidewalks around the store. Murray wouldn't let me." It hurts all of us to think that Nathan and Ida were so sad because they weren't allowed to work. They clearly felt left out, marginalized, and no longer needed.

While it is true that Murray tried to restrict Nathan and Ida from working in their later years, he only did so because he thought it was in their best interest. He didn't realize at the time that all they wanted to do was to continue to work. Later, Murray expressed misgivings and remorse about his efforts to change their lifestyle. He truly felt he was doing his mother and father a favor.

However, it was later apparent to both my parents that the way in which Nathan and Ida were asked to take time for themselves after close to sixty years of working side by side at Nathan's in Coney Island may not have been the best idea. But my father had seen his mom and dad overwork during their entire lives and simply wanted them to enjoy some time for themselves. To Murray, that meant more than going to work till the day they died. It actually meant developing some other interests.

Who is to say what is the best way to spend one's time and what makes someone happy? My father and mother learned that the hard way. Today people who have worked most of their lives will continue to do so later in life, even if they can afford to retire, because they want to keep busy and do what makes them happy. I think my mom and dad would have acted differently today. In fact, they may have even suggested that both my grandma and grandpa be allowed to work in some capacity at the store. It is more widely known today that people may need to feel useful in order to uphold the will to live even when they are elderly. Maintaining purpose and a reason to get out of bed each day can often extend lives, but every person is different.

In the post-Nathan era, it could not have been easy for Murray and Sol to step into the void where their father's aura used to prevail over the store. While my grandfather was alive, everyone in the Coney Island store constantly commented about what "the old man" would do or say. Murray and Sol simply could not escape the large shadow he cast. "Nathan this" or "Nathan that" was the usual reference point for line workers and longtime and regular customers.

Despite Nathan's diminutive physical stature (he was only about 5'3" or 5'4"), everyone knew when he was "in the house." Many people feared him as well as Ida, who never spoke much, but you better believe people would listen when she did. Neither my father nor uncle possessed the same fear factor with the employees as their father had.

But of course the business went on without Nathan and Ida being there, just as they would have wanted it to. Eventually I would become an integral part of the business. After graduating college in 1976, I joined Nathan's as a full-time employee and began an intimate journey into the business. It wasn't all rainbows and butterflies. Nathan's had a dark side, and when I joined the team I learned what was really going on inside the family business, recognized my own strengths and weaknesses, and developed my own work ethic fueled by a near tragedy in my family.

*Section 3*

# RIDING THE
# MERRY-GO-ROUND
### 1970's – 1980's

Chapter 5

# A Higher Education

*E*ven before college began I questioned myself about needing to attend all four years of school when I knew I was going to work at Nathan's. I had awaited the opportunity to work at Nathan's full-time for my entire life. But my parents strongly advised me to go to college and get a liberal arts education and enjoy exposure to many different subjects.

## College and Courtship

I took their advice to heart and landed at Ithaca College. During my years there, I ended up enjoying a variety of courses. I found many excellent teachers and learned a tremendous amount about myself, like what motivates me and other people, and how to live a positive life. Besides the academic benefit, I believe college should help people obtain a better understanding of their belief systems and core values, while exposing them to a variety of unique experiences, and enabling them to meet new people and form relationships that could last a lifetime. Just as Nathan's offered customers a variety of foods to enjoy, college allowed me to sample plenty of different tastes and figure out what I actually loved to be involved with in the future.

But the best thing about college, and what changed my life the most, was meeting my future wife, Amy Thalheim. Professor Pat Pesoli-Bishop (my English professor) and her husband, Dr. Jeffrey Bishop (Amy's psychology professor), conspired to make that happen. Pat was the toughest teacher I had, but she taught me how to write and express myself, which has helped me throughout life. I had enjoyed two or three courses with her when she invited me to her downtown off campus home for a cup of coffee and a chat during my sophomore year. It was not unusual for some students to get together at her home with her and her husband, whom I had met several times before. This was an informal way of exploring different perspectives on the class and on life in a more relaxed atmosphere. At the same time, Jeff invited Amy over, suggesting she come to the house to review her paper. Their real agenda was to introduce us to one another. Funny enough, they didn't want to talk about school at all.

Amy and I started to date steadily the spring semester of my sophomore year and Amy's freshman year. At the same time, I was thinking about leaving school and starting work. I was very interested in developing my relationship with Amy, but my desire to leave school in my junior year was greater at the time. I discussed with Amy my feelings about having to pursue a different course of action instead of continuing school. My parents and a few teachers with whom I had a close relationship sat down with me to brainstorm how I might start my Nathan's career while continuing my path toward a college degree.

Since I could see graduation in sight, they strongly urged me to complete my degree. But they also suggested I take a semester of working at Nathan's while writing papers about my experiences there. I agreed with their idea. This enabled me to continue my education while preparing me for life after college.

Students often took semesters abroad, and it was common for my contemporaries to take advantage of all sorts of opportunities away from campus before returning to finish their senior year. This proposition seemed like an invigorating way to learn more about Nathan's management for the first time while still working toward my college degree. It was the best of both worlds. I was overly excited for this innovative experience.

During the work-study program, my responsibilities opened my eyes to the inner workings of being a Nathan's restaurant manager. This was my first experience on the front line as a manager, rather than a counter man or kitchen employee. Many factors like growing up and listening to my parents discussing the nuances of business issues with vendors, locations, shareholders, banking, labor problems, product pricing, marketing, and now working as a manager helped round out my understanding of all operational functions and responsibilities at the store level. This proved vital to my future contributions and to the success of our company.

In addition to my work at Nathan's I had a unique opportunity to take a five week-long externship at one of the most revered restaurants in New York City, The 21 Club. Through the National Restaurant Association and New York Restaurant Association, my father had met the owners/partners of The 21 Club, Jerry Berns and Jack Kriendler. Murray got to know Jerry Berns very well. My parents and the Berns family became friends and enjoyed many dinners together. Murray arranged for me to sit down with Jerry and Jack on different occasions, and they eventually invited me for an internship at the Club.

The time spent at The 21 Club was a once-in-a-lifetime work experience, especially because I was used to working in a fast food environment, not an elegant fine-dining restaurant. I worked there for five weeks, spending one week in each department in the back of the house: receiving, meat department, butchering, prep (including cold salads, working the grill, sautéing), and in the restaurant's bakery.

It was a wonderful experience. I rented a small apartment in a house next to the Long Island railroad station and took the 4:30 a.m. train, then the subway to West 52$^{nd}$ Street, close to where the restaurant was located. On most days, I'd be the only one in my subway car. I had to knock on the side kitchen door when I reached the restaurant so a night watchman would let me in. I felt privileged to have this opportunity, even if the sun was still rising when I exited the subway station.

While working in the bakery, I remember the baker had to come up with a unique dessert based on the theme of the original *Great Gatsby* movie, which had just been released. He came up with a recipe requiring layers of whipped cream, caramel, and chocolate mousse. He called it something like "The Gatsby Gold Coast Parfait." I helped set up a hundred of these on trays for the movie's release celebration.

When I worked on the grill during a lunch period an expeditor called out the orders to all stations. I was tasked with throwing steaks on the grill. One day while Jerry Berns's wife was dining there she ordered a rare steak. When it arrived, the head chef went to her table to see that everything was prepared to her liking. Five minutes later he came back and banged the counter with a spatula, stomping around and screaming, "She wants the steak more well done!" He was furious that she questioned what a rare steak was and his ability to cook one properly. He went absolutely nuts, even though the customer was the owner's wife. No one messed with him and his kitchen. All I thought was that she just wanted the steak cooked a little more, end of story. Needless to say, I would never question this chef!

Chefs and sous chefs consider everything they do a trade secret. One of the things I enjoyed was watching their use of ingredients. While looking on, I would keep a small journal and write down all that I saw and learned. I always felt that if I focused on the opportunity, I could acquire some valuable information that could be applied to Nathan's in some small way.

Even though the two restaurants were quite different, they both offered high quality food to their customers. I had to watch carefully lest the chef snap at me, "I'm not here to teach you to be a chef; you'd take my job!" By watching them, I acquired a knack for understanding how to elevate an eating experience by adding just a few extra touches to the food. I felt so lucky to work at one of the premier restaurants in the city and enjoyed this fantastic learning opportunity.

**Frank Lesson:** *Listen to those around you, even when they are not talking to you. You never know what you can learn by keeping your ears open and your mouth shut!*

## Returning to School

When I returned to school, I realized how much I missed Amy during the time I was in New York. I wanted to take our relationship to the next level. The feeling was mutual, and after a few months I proposed to her and we got engaged. In fact, we couldn't wait to tie the knot before graduating. In 1975, we married during Christmas break. Amy, studying education, took twenty-one credits in each semester of her junior year just so we could graduate together in 1976. I was amazed and impressed that anyone could do that while maintaining good grades and graduating magna cum laude.

After over four decades of marriage, Amy and I still stay in touch with Pat, who introduced us to one another. We feel we owe our life together to Pat and her late husband Jeff, two very important people. Pat and Jeff recognized something in each of us and knew that we would be a good match for each other. Obviously, they were correct. We will forever be in their debt.

> **Frank Lesson:** *Remember to keep in touch with people who have impacted and helped guide you through life. You never know when they won't be around.*

## Walking into a Firestorm

After graduating, when I was in the office setting, I was not afraid to get my hands dirty with hard work. Even so, I was not necessarily prepared for what I was to experience during my first couple of years on the job.

Before I joined on a full-time basis, my oldest brother, Steve, had already left the company a couple of years before. He was in charge of monitoring product specifications during his tenure at the company. I was aware that he used to go to the stores and try to work with store management to implement correct product-handling procedures. He told me that *all* of his reports indicated a general refusal to implement product specifications properly. He wrote many memos to the head of operations and copied Murray.

Every month he reported the same outcome: no corrections were implemented. The stores didn't listen to Steve's input or the specification manual, which every store kept on its premises. The store managers made no effort to improve and totally ignored many of the staff's directives. This is just one of many problems I was to inherit. I knew this situation would have to change eventually to one of cooperation, not constant conflict.

During the time while I was both in school and at Nathan's, my middle brother, Kenny, was working for the company in the main office as vice president of development. His involvement with company planning protected him from the front lines of the day-to-day operations. He was spared from fighting with different factions on a daily basis. Ken felt that we needed to create a more future-oriented plan for the company. In speaking with him he told me that his biggest contribution to Nathan's was arranging a company retreat to have planning meetings with both the corporate office and the top operations management personnel to discuss our future company development.

Ken said that many ideas came out of the time spent at the three-day American Management Association (AMA) run event. One major idea that is still in effect today is the concept of selling Nathan's products outside of traditional company and franchised restaurant systems. This idea was always out there, but we felt there were many more basic restaurant development opportunities that needed to be tested before stepping out of the box.

Due to our constant efforts to survive, we were never fully able to hash through all of our thoughts and opportunities back then. In many regards, the concept of the retreat process to discuss our future was great in theory, but the timing was off.

After Kenny took over the marketing function, he did have more daily interactions with operations and became more aware of the financial crisis that was unfolding.

The disdain and lack of cooperation between corporate office management and the operational (store) management escalated after Nathan's 1975 acquisition of Wetson's chain of fast food restaurants, right before I joined the company full-time.

We experienced many bumps in the road. Those bumps became extremely clear to me as I enjoyed my new found role in the company while still focusing on my studies. But that was not my only experience during the course of that semester.

## The Wetson's Effect

As mentioned earlier, Nathan's changed substantially once we acquired Wetson's. One of the big problems of the merger was integrating the Wetson's organization into Nathan's system—both in terms of physical stores and employee training. The acquisition of the Wetson's restaurants in the tri-state area included a handful of successful fast food locations, but also many more near-failing ones. Instead of cherry-picking the best units, we purchased the majority of the open stores. This decision almost cost our company its life.

From the very beginning, our approach to management structure was flawed. We separated our restaurants into two divisions: the original Nathan's restaurants that we dubbed "full-line" stores, and the smaller, converted Wetson's units that we called "compact" stores. We experienced a lot of aggravation before realizing the restaurants were all Nathan's, with only one operating mission. So we did away with the labeling and transformed into one chain of restaurants with no division in name or reality. Harold and Wayne Norbitz, and many others who had been part of senior management at Wetson's joined the Nathan's team.

Unfortunately, my father listened to some close advisors whose concept for the Wetson's purchase seemed to make good business sense at the time. Our expansion into the metro area would introduce more customers to the Nathan's brand and increase overall sales. This would be due to the penetration and cost efficiency of our advertising.

Their concept hinged on successful implementation of three major factors:

1. We had enough money for a large-scale and effective marketing and advertising campaign.
2. The restaurants would be in the right locations.
3. The products, service methodology, and local consumers would positively receive the overall customer experience.

The problem with the first factor was that we could not overcome the other two issues, even if we had flawlessly implemented a marketing plan with an unlimited marketing budget. Even though internally we stopped differentiating between the stores, Nathan's found it difficult to develop commercials that would resonate with the new stores' more limited menus versus the full-line menus in the larger and older stores. We could truly only develop a campaign around franks and fries.

This presented a problem because, in addition to our high-quality franks and fries, menu diversity was our major competitive advantage. But the Wetson's locations were too small to manage our full menu. Therefore, any media campaign based on menu diversity would not be very practical and likely would be counterproductive.

The company borrowed two million dollars to convert all the Wetson's restaurants to Nathan's. But we had to spread that money throughout scores of stores. We could only afford to make superficial efforts to transform Wetson's locations into Nathan's restaurants. We slapped a new exterior coat of paint onto many of the locations; repainted the interior; installed some limited new equipment; and developed new promotional signage and limited menu boards. It was pretty much the bare essentials. There was no space in the newly renovated stores to incorporate the full menu found in previous Nathan's locations. As a result, and in terms of the competition, our only differentiators were the high-quality franks and fries, our obvious signature items.

We would have needed additional capital had we chosen to push a major media campaign for any sustained length of time. We expected to rely heavily on cash flow from the newly converted stores to provide capital for the marketing campaign. That cash flow never materialized, further hampering our ability to run a major ongoing campaign.

As for the second factor regarding location of the stores, we quickly found those stores that were successful as Wetson's were very successful as Nathan's. The inverse was also true. If the store was a loser at a Wetson's location, it was unlikely that slapping on a new name would make any difference. We could have afforded to build newly designed Nathan's restaurants from scratch if we had just cherry-picked the best Wetson's locations and not purchased the others. Hindsight is a wonderful thing. Lesson learned: location, location, and of course, location.

During my years in the restaurant business, one thing I gleaned was how to become a better operator by learning from the competition. McDonald's was the premier operator. Even though it has menu issues today, it remains the role model for efficient fast food execution. Its operational systems were and still are the best. And if any fast food company could adapt to the marketing needs of the consumer, McDonald's could do so.

> **Frank Lesson:** *Competition forces people to operate at a higher level and to meet or exceed the competitor's experience.*

Nathan always told my father, and my father told my brothers and me, that competition pushes the envelope and will motivate you to become a better business operator. My grandfather's marketing concept was a simple one: "Give 'em and let them eat" the best possible product for the best possible price. The highest quality frankfurter and french fries are my family's legacy, one that I upheld during all the years I worked at the company. Nathan's Famous has capitalized on this premise and understands that the food is what made Nathan's truly "famous."

Fortunately, we were able to sell several less successful company-owned locations to mom-and-pop franchisees, because they were small enough to buy themselves a job and make a little extra profit. These marginally successful operations were not viable for the company to make enough money on, but local franchise owners could make a go of them because they had less overhead and responsibility. Instead of hiring a general manager, the operators could serve as hands-on general managers and live off any profit created. We subleased the properties and equipment packages to these new franchisees, which reduced our operational expenses and real estate exposure for the short term.

But it wasn't always so easy. These local franchised stores had long-term problems. For instance, when they needed to renovate the property or update the operations, there were no guarantees they'd have the capital to do so.

Ultimately, they would have to close the store because they couldn't break even in these situations.

Finally, as to the third factor, the limited menu disappointed the expectations of some local customers of the renovated compact stores because they lacked variety. These diners expected to see a larger, Coney Island-style menu. In addition, the restaurants were still drab, with Wetson's original 1950s construction and design. We could only do so much. In many of the locations, we failed to meet customers' expectations, to the point that nothing could save some of the stores.

However, the successfully converted stores overcame the menu shortcomings. In these stores, additional offerings that matched local needs supplemented the basic menu. The local store managers and their operations supervisors were both responsible to determine exactly which changes and menu additions were needed, as it was their success that was on the line.

*Wetson's restaurant conversion, Stamford, CT, 1976*
*Photo credit: Bill Mitchell Photography*

Even if Nathan's could have implemented the three factors required to make the Wetson's acquisition successful, divisiveness within Nathan's management team and between Nathan's management and the inherited Wetson's executives prevented the merger from initially succeeding.

It was impossible for me, or anyone for that matter, to escape the effects of management's backstabbing and mistrust, especially between the full line and compact operations teams. A prime example occurred during one of the Wetson's restaurant conversions, when a full line Nathan's employee proved himself to be nothing but trouble.

Typically, both operations personnel would come to help open a store. In this instance, a compact operations management executive, several years after the fact, relayed a story to me. He said with just five minutes before a newly converted store was ready to open its doors, with a huge number of customers stretched in a long line around the block, he saw a Nathan's full line employee pull the fire-suppression system (the extinguisher system above the fryers). Of course the employee's actions completely disrupted the opening and stressed staff and line personnel even beyond the normal anxiety of a new store's opening day. Worse, many employees passed down to others their prevailing disrespect for the people from Wetson's. It was behavior like this that showed the extensive problems within our company.

However, not all was lost during this time of dysfunction. During my first year as a full-time employee, one bright spot in the marketing department was the opportunity to serve as a judge for the annual Fourth of July hot dog eating contest in Coney Island.

## Hot Dog Eating Contest Rolls Around

From a marketing perspective, Nathan's hot dog eating contest was and still is a public relations homerun event for the company. The Nathan's official website (nathansfamous.com) says that "according to legend," the very first contest dates back to the year of the company's founding: 1916. Some sources claim the contest, which is held at our flagship Coney Island store, actually began after we hired Mortimer Matz and his partner Max Rosey to handle our publicity.

Max Rosey was the founder of the event. I remember him as a lovable, Runyon-esque character who exuded constant enthusiasm. No matter the size of the project, he'd take it to the limit. Whether it was a single store opening or the largest hot dog eating contest in the world, he devoted the same energy and devotion to ensuring it was a fantastic event. He told me how he thought of this very simple yet memorable marketing event for Nathan's.

In addition to Nathan's, Max also represented a large department store in Allentown, Pennsylvania, called Hess's Department Stores. At that company, he had an idea to run a donut-eating contest, and it proved to be successful. So naturally he thought that our hosting a hot dog eating contest would bring much more attention to us than the donuts ever did for Hess's. He had no idea how his idea would live on and grow into an international bonanza so many years after his death in 1991!

When given the chance, Max didn't take credit for launching the contests. Rather, he supposedly spoke about the event and told reporters that Eddie Cantor and Mae West's father were finalists in that first 1916 contest. He was obviously more interested in hyping the company than in personal acclaim. Maxie also claimed that during the 1920s, Babe Ruth regularly won Nathan's contest "by acclaim." But although the Babe was known as an avid hot dog fan, it's unlikely that the Yankees would have released him from right field during their regular Independence Day game to chow down on Nathan's finest.

To this day, the hot dog eating contest remains a huge winner. People always ask me about the hot dog eating contest. The contest is a major media-marketing phenomenon, though not at the level of events like baseball's World Series or football's Super Bowl. Nor can the company measure the effect of the event on national sales of all of Nathan's supermarket or restaurant products. However, this event is one that a very persistent PR man started as a stunt, and it brings tens of thousands of spectators and the press to Coney Island and the restaurant every Fourth of July, which usually is an otherwise slow news day. Additionally, the contest results in plenty of print, radio, TV, and Internet media attention from around the world.

In this book about the history of Nathan's Famous, I want to clear up a few things about the origins of the contest. At the time Max Rosey first conceptualized the event, the contest was just a minor PR stunt, and not at the level of the current marketing effort we now see every Fourth of July. He and Mortimer Matz, who oversaw many major political campaigns in Manhattan, were huge fans of Nathan, Murray, and the company. In fact, Max came to live and breathe the Nathan's business.

The early contests would last ten minutes, and the contestants would eat maybe fifteen to twenty hot dogs on a good day. Early in the morning on the day of the event, Max would come down to the store to ensure management set up a few eight-foot tables with red, white, and blue bunting and hang as many Nathan's banners around the area as possible. This would guarantee the Nathan's logo was visible in all the pictures that appeared in the newspapers or on television.

In an effort to gather a dozen or so people for the contest, Max would run around outside the store about an hour before the event, asking people who were just milling around if they'd want to eat some free hot dogs. His main job, for weeks before the contest, was to make sure the major networks, local and public television stations, newspapers and radio stations would be present to cover the event. He would call reporters dozens of times a day, asking, "You guys are coming, right?" He would even go down to the stations and editors' desks of newspapers to stay on top of them and make sure they sent the reporters to cover the event.

Max was more than a bit "crazy-smart" but also probably one of the most disorganized people I had ever seen. You couldn't walk into his cubicle at our headquarters because his stacks of papers and pictures cluttered the floor and every surface. However, he knew where everything was…eventually! Whenever I would ask him for something, he'd say, "I'll come to you when I find it." Everyone loved Max because they knew that he was completely dedicated, pulling out all the stops to get positive Nathan's stories published.

**Frank Lesson:** *Hire innovative people with fire in their belly. They will help you be more creative and possibly be the difference in making your business usher in success with new ideas.*

Max started to slow down in 1988. He took in a young man, George Shea, who helped turn this small annual contest into a nationally televised event. Every word George utters about Max communicates his abiding respect for Max Rosey and what he stood for as a PR guy. George credits Max with teaching him what makes a good public relations person. These lessons include:

- Focus on creative ways to promote the event rather than on how much money you can make off the client.
- Figure out what will elicit the most excitement for the event.
- Be engaged in the game.
- Consider how to arrange all the puzzle pieces to make the event run as smoothly and effectively as possible.

Max and George exemplified the above lessons in implementing the Hot Dog Eating contest program for Nathan's. The crowning jewel is the Annual Nathan's Famous 4th of July Hot Dog eating contest at Coney Island. They perfected every aspect of the promotion and excitement of the event. Tens' of thousands of spectators are drawn every year to the Coney Island event and are entertained by George Shea. The audience who watch it unfold on television are treated to extra special feature stories about the contestants by the ESPN announcers prior to the actual start of the contest. It is a great experience for all who have the opportunity to watch it!

Wayne had told me that he made the decision to make changes to the format of the contest once George became involved. They moved the contest to the corner of Surf and Stillwell and created the greater role of the MC during the contest. George's personality definitely took the contest to a new level. While America enjoyed eating contests for years before Nathan's came along, the fact that Nathan's Famous hot dog eating contest became the granddaddy of all competitive eating contests is no accident. George's efforts took the event to new heights, sparking national interest in this annual festival. George created the "Mustard Champion Belt" which he would hand out to the winner at the end of the annual event.

In 1997 and 1998, after a Japanese man named Hirofumi Nakajima won the contest both years, George created additional PR by demanding that someone get the Mustard Belt back to the USA. He then came up with a great statement and gave further attention to the event by shouting to the world that the contest is "The litmus test of American patriotism!" and "We must bring the belt home again!" However, it wasn't until another Japanese individual came along that the competition became the world-renowned event it is today.

In 2001, Takeru Kobayashi transformed the contest by doubling the number of dogs he downed from a world record of 25 ½ to 50. From 2001 to 2006, he won six consecutive competitions. Kobayashi, a 5'8", 128-pound 22-year-old from Japan, developed creative techniques such as breaking each frank in two

*The stage for the 2015 main event*
*Photo Credit: Paul Martinka*

and eating both halves at the same time (known as "the Solomon" technique, named after the biblical King's threat), eating the buns separately after first dunking them in water to make them go down more easily than dry buns would, and shaking his body as he stuffed his face to help digest the dogs more quickly.

Since 2007 and through 2014, Joey Chestnut reigned supreme as the champ of the Nathan's contests. In 2013, he set the current record of sixty-nine franks and has yet to best his personal and world record. But in 2015 Matt Stonie emerged as the winner, consuming 62 hot dogs to Chestnut's 60.

In 2003, ESPN aired the contest for the first time. Since 2005, Paul Page has called the play-by-play, accompanied by color commentator Richard Shea. The cable station typically lures one to two million viewers during each contest. In 2014, ESPN signed an agreement to carry the competition until 2024.

*A new champion is crowned.*
*Photo Credit: Paul Martinka*

In 2004, the company erected a three-story-high "Hot Dog Eating Wall of Fame" at the site of the annual contest. The wall lists past winners and features a digital clock that counts down the minutes until the next contest. In 2007, an estimated fifty thousand spectators headed to Coney Island to witness the competition.

But the competition is not just limited to men. Women used to participate along with the men until 2011 when Sonya Thomas won the inaugural women's competition and its "bejeweled" Pink Belt. The winner of the men's competition is given possession of the coveted international Mustard Belt. Various other prizes have been awarded over the years. For example, in 2004 Orbitz donated a travel package to the winner. Since 2007, winners of both the men's and women's divisions each began taking home cash prizes of $10,000, with the second-place finishers earning $5,000. Third-, fourth-, and fifth-place finishers respectively receive $2,500, $1,500, and $1,000.

Today there are many eating contests in cities around the country and around the globe, including China, Japan, and Russia. Max Rosey would be proud of how George Shea developed his concept into its current historic level of PR success. In terms of the company's marketing efforts and budget, this event has become Nathan's major annual publicity program.

And as I mentioned above, acting as a judge in 1976 and 1977 was a highlight of my early months working in the marketing department. But, I knew that job was not the best fit for me after serving in that position.

## Earning My Stripes

One issue always haunted me even when I worked at Nathan's as a kid during vacations: nepotism. That motivated me to prove myself, although initially doing so turned out to be almost impossible. But it wasn't for any lack of trying. At the age of twenty-one, when my father assigned me to my first full-time, permanent job as manager of marketing, I simply lacked the expertise that the position demanded. Right from the start, this caused trouble for me.

At the time, I knew diddly-squat about marketing. I still have a sample of my first project, in which I made bumper stickers with "Mr. Frankie" that read, "Frankie says: If you can read this, you're too close." These were to be given out as a premium to customers for coming into the store. In retrospect, this was an expensive item that didn't bring customers into the stores and had no positive effect on sales at a time when we desperately needed to bring bodies to the counter. But I tried my best. I had to learn how to do the best job possible and help the restaurants bring in sales, even though I was never formally trained in marketing or advertising.

In 1977, and after nine months or so, things came to a head. Wayne (then director of operations for the compact stores) and I had a conversation. When I asked him if I was meeting the marketing needs for the stores, he said to me, "Listen, I respect you. You work hard, you're trying hard, you know the operations. But what do you know about marketing?" I always had a good relationship with Wayne. We were always on the same page as to the direction of the company and shared the same visions and priorities for accomplishing our goals. His response brought to light what I already knew. The company needed an experienced person in the marketing position—and I was not it.

Most employees might have been too afraid of the repercussions of being so brutally honest. They might have felt, "He's the boss's son, how could I talk to him that way?" But Wayne focused on the best interests of the company and didn't fear the consequences of being forthright or speaking up about problems.

> **Frank Lesson:** *Find employees who are willing to speak the truth and provide honest feedback, even if it is not exactly what you want to hear.*

Wayne's comments didn't insult me in the least. If anything, I felt relieved. I always wanted to get sales to the bottom line because the most important thing was to help the company. So I told my father that the marketing position was not right for me. At first he told me, "You're bright, you understand the business; you can do this." But I dug my heels in and said, "No, I'm not good enough at marketing for what the company needs; I belong in operations."

He respected my passion and feelings about the job function that would best help me to grow and contribute, and he found another position for me that better suited my expertise: working under the purchasing and corporate food service department with the title of director of supermarket sales. My duties included heading the budding supermarket licensing program. The company signed a deal with a frankfurter manufacturer to produce and sell our hot dogs for sale in supermarkets for guaranteed annual royalty fees. This job was in conjunction with working in the purchasing department—and all the functions associated with it.

As excited as I was about my new position, I made some painful mistakes in my first weeks and months there.

## Painful Lessons

In my first couple of years at Nathan's, one pivotal and very painful learning experience came with the then vice president of operations. At least one day a week, I was tasked with going to each store to see how management was handling product, just as my brother Steve had done for several years before. Additionally, I visited vendors to see how they handled our products and to get a feel for industry standards.

On one occasion, I made the rounds with an operations supervisor and asked him his opinion about his boss, the operations vice president. My question got back to that vice president, who was passively-aggressively furious with me. When I got back to the home office the next day, the vice president cornered me and said, "I understand you were asking about me. If you have a problem with me, you can talk to me directly."

I felt like crawling under my desk. I sensed a destructive negative culture pervading the company. Instead of a single harmonious company, there was a prevailing behavioral norm of people undercutting one another and not working toward the common goal of success. In my own mind, I was not trying to "get dirt" on the vice president. Rather, I was just trying to understand the company's transition from a full-line menu restaurant chain to incorporating new fast food-type compact stores with more limited menus.

To obtain these goals, I felt the employees' opinions of leadership surely mattered. I wanted to know how much cooperation existed between current management team members and the newly expanded management team, which headed the conversions of Wetson's into Nathan's restaurants. Because this company was my lifeblood, I felt a duty to evaluate from an outside perspective exactly how the current ops vice president (who had been with Nathan's for more than twenty years) got along with a management team member from Wetson's.

Only after the fact did I realize that by inquiring about his boss, I had put that employee in a precarious position. How did he know I wasn't setting him up and going to report back to the vice president if he made negative comments? The culture was really out of sync. There was little trust. This type of culture was not conducive to a successful operations team, and the lack of synergy was eating away at the company's potential.

Even worse than my embarrassment was my realization of how unhealthy this attitude was for the company. I talked to Murray about the spread of negativity. He was not happy about the situation, but nothing changed to improve these hostile attitudes for several years.

Reporting to the then vice president of purchasing wasn't a great experience for me either. While the job itself was a good fit, my boss perceived me as a threat. Since I was the son of the company leader, his resentment stemmed from nepotism. Unlike my boss, the other people in the department had

*William at the office*
*Photo credit: Handwerker Family collection*

no problems with me because they recognized that I had a lot to learn, and my only goal was to roll up my sleeves to acquire as much knowledge and experience as possible.

I listened to all the conversations department staff had with store management, vendors, operational supervisory management, and main office personnel. But the vice president of purchasing could not see past his close-minded perception that I had been handed my position on a silver platter. It is true that I got the job and my name is Handwerker. However, I felt that this job was something that I knew through my years working in operations from the bottom up. I would be very committed to doing what was needed for the company for many years to come.

I started to obtain a better sense of what was wrong in operations. No matter what the industry or level of intelligence of the employees, there's a learning curve in every job. It took me over a year to identify the majority of problems from within and to find opportunities to improve the operations. With all the company's concurrent expansion programs, there were many issues that needed to be addressed. What troubled me most was the dysfunctional internal fighting at various management levels, as well as between the home office and stores.

The prevailing contempt by existing employees of Nathan's toward Wetson's top management and store managers seemed unshakable. Some Nathan's managers thought, "What does a bankrupt management team know about operating restaurants compared with our team that's been around for sixty years?" They refused to recognize that Wetson's had some very talented managers and systems, some of which Nathan's successfully adopted over time as standard operating procedures.

The lack of respect persisted between some of the corporate staff and store management, from the older full-line stores and their attitude toward the compact-line of newly converted units. The situation was the reverse of what my brother Steve experienced before he left in 1974. In that case, it was the stores ignoring the needs of management, not the other way around. In this case, management failed to recognize that their role was to serve the restaurants above all else. If the stores weren't successful, the office staff would not get paid. It became clear the existing attitude needed an adjustment.

The operations vice president eventually left the company. Wayne Norbitz took charge of all full-line and compact stores operations after it all came to a head. He created a more coordinated culture. Finally, there was a singular set of directives with only one person in control of operations. Once everyone got on the same page and the undertone of fear and backstabbing dissipated, the entire company knew, accepted, and started following the common mission: The customer is number one. Our business depends on their positive experience in order to make them repeat customers. Teamwork is essential in making that happen!

I learned a lot through all of this: about people, how to act and not to act, and how to be honest and up-front with everyone. I learned not just from my mistakes, but also from my co-workers in the company. For instance, I worked very closely with Harold Norbitz on the contract terms of our supermarket packaged frankfurter licensing deal at the time with John Morrell & Co. Harold taught me several negotiation techniques and tactics I have never forgotten, and which I continue to use in all of my business and even personal negotiations.

These included my personal favorites like:

- The negotiator should always have a knowledgeable colleague present during the negotiating process to look, listen, and make your side of the table appear less vulnerable. Toward the last round of negotiations, bring an attorney.
- But attorneys should not do your negotiating. It's up to the businessmen and women to do that. After all, nobody knows the objective better than the businessperson. Attorneys are there to point out any risks and ensure that your rights are protected. Then the businessperson should evaluate what they're willing to risk.
- Insist that your attorney draft the initial agreement and spell out your position, even though you incur additional legal fees. It's up to the other party to point out any problems or objections.
- Negotiations should create a "win-win" for both parties. No long-term relationship can really succeed unless both parties benefit. But this does not mean that either party must cave in on crucial issues that protect his

or her respective long-term needs; it just means we can all do well in a negotiation.

In our licensing negotiations, our primary concern was to ensure that we had trademark protection on all fronts: final manufacturing approval on any and all product specifications that would bear our trademark logo, liability insurance protection limits, and marketing programs. The royalty structure had to include guaranteed monies with annual increases. It was very important that the company be incentivized to promote the product line.

We hoped that by requiring an annual increase in our minimum guaranteed royalty structure, we would motivate Morrell to try its best to increase sales. Whether they sold more licensed hot dogs or not, our annual royalties were guaranteed to increase to ensure they'd remain motivated to pull out all the stops to increase sales.

One of the contentious issues that we held onto strongly was our ability to legally demand that Morrell recall our products if we felt the situation was dire enough to do so. It was of utmost importance to protect our brand and trademark. We had to have the final right to make that decision, and it was non-negotiable for our company and our attorneys. Finally, language was developed and accepted by both parties.

Throughout the late 1970s and early 1980s, I grew more capable of helping the company get through its troubled times. As I continued to learn the business from the inside out, I became part of the restructuring process to position Nathan's on the right path for future growth and stability.

## Inside Out

During our company's tremendous turmoil in the early 1980s, I saw my father juggling multiple crises and constantly snuffing out huge fires like dealing with the pressures from shareholders, the press, and internecine bickering among management. Simultaneously, in-house and external advisors pulled him in many different directions with conflicting suggestions. Murray's drive to succeed when all looked bleak was his strong suit. He would never succumb to the pressure. Some people would have taken the easier path in resolving the difficult issues.

Looking back, I can't imagine how he handled going public, opening new company-owned stores, initiating franchising, licensing hot dogs and other Nathan's branded products, and acquiring Wetson's, especially when these initiatives took a great deal of time to produce any tangible returns. Entering just one of these arenas would have been a huge leap for any one person bred in the backdrop of a relatively small family operation. It was a herculean task to take them on all at once.

Many of these projects got off to shaky starts. But he never indicated his discouragement to me or that he had misgivings about his decisions. He never quit, which says a lot about his focus, endurance, and unshakable vision and ambition. In fact, when the company hit its low point around 1981, he could easily have taken the company through Chapter 11 bankruptcy, enabling him to wipe the slate clean of debts and get the company on surer footing. But he had too much integrity to leave vendors and creditors high and dry by resorting to the easy way out.

Many people thought this was a mistake, but my dad was adamant about his decision. If at all possible, he would not allow our family legacy to include a Nathan's Famous Chapter 11 bankruptcy. Although we did come close to resorting to it, Murray eventually persevered.

Once I joined the company full-time, my father often confided in me. This was both eye opening and confusing. I felt honored that he trusted me with such sensitive information and discussed the pressures he faced; yet, I was often frustrated that I had so few insights and little help to offer because I was so green. What did I know? What could I possibly do with this information but worry about my father, the company, and my own job security?

## Chapter 6

# Saving Nathan's: The Plan

*A*s the 1975 Wetson's merger drained Nathan's financial resources, the company scrambled for several years to dig out of debt and return to profitability. Some efforts would prove successful. However, we traversed a very troubled road.

Starting around 1978, and after all the conversions were complete, it was apparent that returns were not flowing in as expected. Despite the Nathan's Famous name and logo on the sides of the marginally converted Wetson's stores, the bad locations came very close to putting us out of business.

We were trimming expenses wherever we could. We even ordered the bare minimum supplies to reduce costs and preserve our cash flow. It got so bad that if a recently renovated store's three garbage cans were getting old and battered, we'd order three new ones, but not just for that store. We'd transfer one from the set to the newer stores for their parking lot (where customers might see it) and then tell the manager at that store, "You're not going to get the three that you ordered, you can only get one." Then we took his old but usable garbage cans and transferred them to an older, less profitable store, whose garbage cans were falling apart. The newer store's old cans were better than the less profitable store's old garbage cans, and while we would have liked to have only new, clean barrels at every store, we had to be selective and preserve vital resources.

Another example of our cost cutting was that we normally ordered two cases of light bulbs for each store, but instead we would order just one. We would buy another case when it was needed in two weeks to control cash flow demand on small wares. We were watching every dime we spent. I worked with the small vendors and the controller; my father worked with the big vendors. We were in survival mode, going week to week.

I remember sitting in Murray's office after I had several conversations with our vendors who were owed tens of thousands of dollars. Murray and I knew to never promise anyone anything that we couldn't deliver. We would negotiate with vendors, asking for more credit or time to pay our bills. Sometimes we would say, "I can't pay you this week; let's talk this time next week." Or, "I can get you a couple hundred dollars this week and pay the rest in a week or two." This was business "nuts and bolts" and thankfully it worked.

Figuring out how to survive was a valuable lesson, and one I never took for granted. We did what we had to do when our backs were up against the wall. Our ability to work smarter, leaner, and with more effective decision making helped to change us forever.

Murray's drive to succeed when all looked bleakest was his strong suit. One of his greatest accomplishments was to see that the company survived the worst of times using a dignified and honest approach in dealing with any situation. His leadership allowed us to move forward to great heights in the future.

> **Frank Lesson:** *Always be honest and forthcoming with your business partners. It is these relationships that support your business.*

Over time we ended up closing and selling many of the leases or the properties themselves. But even these actions were not enough for us to meet our financial loan covenants or to hold off the banks. Ultimately we had to take several drastic initiatives to improve our situation. One such effort was reconsidering the idea of selling a new line of skinless hot dogs.

## Natural Casing versus Skinless

Management was often concerned about the skinless product ever since we first got into packaged franks in 1976. Initially we failed to appreciate the benefits of offering skinless hot dogs. We first started selling packaged franks to supermarkets with a local manufacturer, Marathon Enterprises (not the current packagers, John Morrell & Co.).

From day one, Marathon told us that the greatest sales, on a retail-packaged basis, are in skinless franks. The price to the consumer is the main reason why. This product's price advantage over natural casing derives from cost savings in the manufacturing process. But Nathan's worried that consumers would reject the skinless franks. We also thought they wouldn't get the "snap" when they bit into them. When the natural casing frank comes off the grill nice and hot, the juices from the first bite explode into the mouth. It is possible to make the skinless franks snap, but it's harder to produce and it will never be exactly the same.

For many years we wouldn't allow the manufacturer to sell Nathan's skinless hot dogs. But several years later, skinless frankfurters ended up being a very important part of our business. Switching to Morrell helped us to see the light. They also were strongly opinionated that putting our name on a skinless product would be a homerun. They were right.

I was among Nathan's managers who initially didn't grasp the significance of what skinless could mean on many different fronts. We reconsidered our position after Morrell came to us and claimed, "We can sell this packaged product and create a national brand because of our manufacturing and marketing abilities." We were impressed and more inclined to listen to Morrell's advice because they were selling to every major chain in the country and even had the distribution set up to handle the expansion.

At the time, Hugo Slotkin was the main contact at John Morrell. In the 1920s and 1930s, when his father worked at HyGrade, another manufacturer of hot dogs, he was one of the suppliers who did business with my grandfather. Hugo pointed out that price-conscious consumers could not afford our natural casing franks, but would be more inclined to buy the skinless as a staple. While these customers may have purchased Nathan's natural casing franks on a special occasion, they regularly did not do so. But it wasn't until 1978 that Hugo finally convinced Murray to enter into a licensing deal.

While the terms were different, the spirit of the agreement was similar to the thinking the Marathon management had discussed a few years prior. But it was the sheer scope of Morrell's reach that persuaded us to consummate a deal that would have otherwise not occurred with Marathon's guidance.

Since the manufacturing process for natural casing hot dogs is more labor intensive, they are more expensive to produce. Essentially they have to be

*A typical day at the frankfurter grill, Coney Island, 1967-1968*
*Photo Credit: Bill Mitchell Photography*

handmade because natural casings are only so long and very fragile. Employees on the manufacturing line have to be gentle and skilled. Substantial waste still occurs even with these skilled employees at the helm, since the casings often break and have to be discarded. As a result, the process of manufacturing casing franks requires multiple shifts of highly trained workers to handle the production of thousands of pounds of these franks.

In contrast, when manufacturing skinless franks, the hot dog meat formulation can be continuously fed through a machine, requiring minimum labor capable of dealing with a larger production of hundreds of thousands of pounds of frankfurters.

As a result, on a retail level, a package of eight Nathan's skinless hot dogs sells for less than a package of five or six natural casing franks. Because there is little perceived difference by consumers, the majority of the public will often choose the skinless option. Some grocery stores don't even sell natural casing packages because they are too expensive.

The manufacturer originally customized a vacuum package to maintain the form of the natural casing hot dogs. While it's a slightly more expensive package, its unique design makes it stand out in the supermarket case and simultaneously keeps the integrity of the frankfurters' shape.

Another concern that fed our initial resistance to selling skinless franks was the belief that customers just wouldn't perceive them to be a Nathan's product because of our perception of their eating expectation. We failed to appreciate the power of our brand. The reality is that, in the eyes of the consumer, what we put in a Nathan's package would be a Nathan's hot dog. At the end of the day, the consumer's opinion was more important than our own.

Still, many of us (including myself) had to move past our own pet peeves and preferences and realize that although we deviated from selling the original natural casing frankfurter, we still made a high-quality product with the same Nathan's standards. Our original beef and spice recipe was so special and tasted so much better than anything else around. So we had perceived that making changes, even small ones, could damage the biggest advantage we had over other hot dog makers, but it didn't, the public, pardon the pun, relished both products.

To me, that's just one example of the true difference between our products and our competitors' products. To understand the difference, please decide for yourself! In fact, my mother loved the skinless frank better than the natural casing, further supporting the notion that the consumer is the most important person to make happy, especially when that person is your mother!

> **Frank Lesson:** *Understand the power of your brand. It may even surprise you.*

When we first started designing the packaging, we realized the power of the Nathan's brand. Initially the experts presented us with various colored designs. The first round of samples had brown labels affixed with the Nathan's logo. But Murray was adamant that we use our green and yellow logo colors on the packaged skinless franks. The so-called "packaging marketing experts" advised us that we could not use green in the supermarket. It had never been done before because the designers assumed consumers would associate that color with moldy meat and not buy the package. We stood by Murray and insisted on using our colors, and eventually we proved the experts wrong.

The manufacturer, distributors, and supermarket managers were shocked that consumers did not balk at the color. To the contrary, the color worked in our favor. Amid the lineup of hot dogs in the aisle, the Nathan's package stood out from the other hot dog packages at each supermarket. We recognized an instant hit by sticking to our marketing colors and consumer-brand awareness in New York. After that, our distributors had no problem selling the product outside the metro area because they were able to use the New York experience to show potential supermarket chains an example of their success.

When we finally decided to take the plunge into a skinless frank, our dire financial circumstances began to turn around. We still joke today that the addition of skinless hot dogs literally helped save our skins on two fronts: in the supermarkets and in the restaurants.

## Supermarket Licensing

Once we agreed on the skinless concept for the licensing deal, I was responsible for managing the supermarket program because of my extensive knowledge of the product. I will never forget this experience.

Overseeing this relationship was my most valuable contribution to the licensing program. My duties included inspecting all manufacturing facilities, working on specifications of product formulations, and making sure they were properly implemented so that the product turned out the way it should. From time to time I handled any consumer issues that arose as a result of product problems, marketing issues, etc.

We had one issue with the skinless hot dogs when the program first began. That is, the production specifications and quality were not up to Nathan's standards. We initially had a tough time approving the final products Morrell produced. The first several batches of both the skinless and natural casing franks had problems. The skinless franks had a slightly bitter taste and we couldn't understand why. Morrell used our formulation as specified. I went to the plant and walked through the manufacturing process with the staff, in hopes of understanding exactly how making a natural casing frank differed from making a skinless one.

It came down to this: making a skinless frank required stuffing the frankfurter emulsion into a synthetic casing, which was cooked in a continuous oven, then cooled down through a cold water shower. The casing would then be peeled off before packaging the product. The shower included a percentage of vinegar within the water. When I asked the plant staff why they used vinegar, they told me that this facilitated in peeling the hot franks from the plastic casing. I realized this was what caused the bitter taste. When I asked Morrell to stop using vinegar, they were able to implement this suggestion with no waste in the production process. The problem was quickly solved.

Initially, the natural casing franks also had production problems, mostly because they were too tough to chew. We found that Morrell over-smoked the franks. Changes in the smoke levels and cooking times and temperatures helped to eliminate the problem.

Another issue occurred when Morrell contended that its spice manufacturer could produce better quality and cheaper products—for both skinless and natural casing—than our specified spice packaging. I totally disagreed. But in the spirit of cooperation, I agreed to test their theory by running a quality test—using me as the taster.

Over the years I came to understand the nuances of all the properties of our name sake product from my father, who learned from my grandfather how to determine a proper Nathan's natural casing frank. I was taught to open the package to see properly consistent sized franks, and feel that the casings were taut, fresh and very light pink or neutral in color.

There were two other major criteria that I would look for before they were even allowed to be cooked, which were that the spice seasoning was correct and that the frankfurter emulsion was not too fatty. To understand if the spice formula and fat content were made to specification, I would take the raw frank and break it half. I would then immediately inhale the aroma. This would allow me to smell if the right concentration of garlic and other seasonings were present. Then I would take bite of the frank to see if it was too fatty by chewing the meat and pressing it to the roof of my mouth. A proper Nathan's frank's fat content would not leave a film of fat on the roof of one's mouth. This testing process took a long time to perfect.

This procedure is ingrained in my sense of smell and taste. It allows me to remember the rich flavors of the meat and the proper strength of the smell of seasonings when I would have broken the frank in half. As I write this passage I can imagine a whiff of the spice formula in my nose, the proper grind of the meat in my mouth, as well as the taste of the garlic and other spices even without having actually executed the test. This is one of the family traditions that was passed on to me. I tried throughout my years on the job to make sure that the product sold to our customers would maintain those standards at all times.

All governmental food agencies recommend that you do not eat unheated processed meats due to the possibility of bacteria that dissipates when reheated. I agree with their recommendation, so do not attempt to try this process in any way.

Morrell's people went on to produce natural casing franks with their proposed spice formula and then a batch with ours. They placed six plates in front of me, with three franks on each plate, labeled A, B, and C. Each plate had a frank with our spice, their spice, and a third spice formulation. They believed the three formulations were so similar that I wouldn't be able to pick out our frank seasoning from the others. But to their surprise, I picked out our frank six out of six times during this "blind taste test." They were shocked and therefore had to agree to use our extremely specific and unique spice packet. I guess my grandmother's spice formula still worked best. After years of being tutored by my grandfather and father on what is a properly processed Nathan's frank, I will always be able to evaluate the product.

Once we got financially back on track through selling our skinless franks in the supermarkets, it was time to start selling the product in our restaurants. At this time, we were just getting by and needed to find a way to increase our sales and reduce costs to remain in business. The first move was to introduce the skinless franks in two of the company stores. During the first several days of sales, we had little to no reaction to the product. This amazed me, but proved that the product was definitely accepted by our loyal customers. It was evident that the taste of our hot dogs were still the best with or without the natural casing!

The skinless franks reduced our overall cost by approximately 2 percent—which may seem minimal but was quite dramatic because the savings fell directly to the bottom line. I was now convinced we had to expand the use of our skinless franks to all the stores we operated.

The supermarket program was doing well, but some of our franchisees were not happy that we were licensing products to supermarkets. Why would anyone patronize a nearby Nathan's franchise if customers could buy our hot dogs at their local supermarket? The threat to the Nathan's restaurant business either company owned or franchised was and still is irrelevant.

But they (and we) had yet to understand that the "purchase intent" is the key to this dilemma. When customers want a snack or meal and they are not at home to cook it, their "purchase intent" is to stop and buy a hot dog and/or french fries at the nearest Nathan's franchise or company restaurant in an airport, stadium, or mall, etc. These are unique captive-market locations where diners want convenience. They are not interested in going home to cook. The upside potential of selling packaged Nathan's franks in the supermarket made complete sense. It didn't stop store growth and it only supported additional sales and the development of the Nathan's brand.

In addition to licensing skinless franks to supermarkets, Murray gave the okay for all company stores (except Coney Island) to sell skinless. We all knew that under no circumstances would Nathan ever want any changes to the original product that he and Ida sold in the founding location. I understood his position, even though we had proved the public accepted the skinless product. However, we would survive without making additional money at Coney Island.

Part of why Coney Island remained so successful throughout all the ups and downs of the company was the good sales they enjoyed. That location was constantly busy, so the *modus operandi* was not as make-or-break as it was at other, less successful locations. Since the bottom line was always there, a lot of things could be off kilter in Coney Island. That's not to say it couldn't have better results, but as management implemented incentives and began supporting the new effective plan, everything fell into place and started to improve.

While sales and profits from our skinless line dramatically increased the company's financial health, the improvement was not enough to offset our debt obligations and completely get the company back on the right track. So we developed another initiative between 1978 and 1980 that further helped prop up the company: couponing. However, that too proved to be a hard sell within Nathan's, as not everyone agreed with the idea.

## Two Faces of Couponing

Remember the old adage that "good sales cure all ills"? This concept applied directly to couponing. During Nathan's roughest time, we badly needed sales. To this day, marketing gurus stand behind the claim that if you don't have an established sales price, you won't be able to get away with an ongoing discounted platform.

The "experts" consider excessive couponing damaging to the marketing of a fast food company or any restaurant operation. The thought is that discounting cheapens the perceived quality of the product line. They insist that if you have no solid marketing stance, you're a discount house that will not attract customers. Why should consumers pay a certain price for a hot dog when they can buy one and then get another one free? When they get a coupon every other week, they will rarely rush to the store but will just wait for the next coupon. That behavior can denigrate the price elasticity and integrity of any retail price structure.

We all knew that raking in revenue was crucial. Wayne, my brother Ken, each store's supervisor, the general manager, and I brainstormed ways to find cost-effective and immediate solutions to the situation. They thought coupons would remind people that the company was still alive and well and hopefully get them through the store doors. Everyone considered the options. Ken likely looked out his thirtieth-floor office window overlooking Times Square and recalled how our grandfather lured customers in the company's earliest years: by undercutting the price.

And so couponing was born. He ordered a hundred thousand coupons for discount hot dogs, and the various restaurant managers hired employees to dole out fliers and coupons in neighborhoods surrounding their stores. Suddenly, new customers and our regular clientele discovered Nathan's bargains and more regularly came to the stores. It's a very delicate balance to implement a coupon program. However, when you are in the position we were in, you need to do whatever you can to drum up revenue.

**Frank Lesson:** *Difficult times call for extreme action. When it comes to survival of the fittest, do what you have to do to prosper.*

The most effective way to get coupons into the customers' hands was not by placing ads in the local papers. It was to get the employees on the street and to have store managers hand them out at schools, local business organizations, and other community groups.

Despite serious questions about the couponing strategy in general, we experimented with different promotions. We ended up printing millions of coupons with several offers: buy three hot dogs for $1.99, buy one get one free (BOGO), or buy one get one for the original price of a nickel. The management of each store would flood his or her local community with these coupons.

We had to carefully consider the blend of offers, how long to keep them going, and how much of a discount to offer. For instance, instead of releasing a "buy one get one free" coupon for one person's meal, we would offer a "three hot dogs for $1.99" coupon which might draw two people, one ordering three hot dogs at the discount and one ordering a dog at full price (so they'd each get two), plus two drinks and an order of fries that they might split.

We had to think long and hard about the profit margin and how to best mix the offers. It wasn't easy to figure out when we should use the coupons and

*"Golden brown all around; how many orders?"*
*yelled out every day to our customers by the counter employees*
*Photo Credit: Bill Mitchell Photography*

when we shouldn't. We were aware that it wouldn't work if we did it every day, especially with the same offer. But in the beginning, we believed sales would increase if we handed out coupons in the right area.

The strategy worked, especially in Times Square where the results were superb. People loved Nathan's, so this tactic drew new clientele and offered existing and former customers an impetus to visit the store. During every lunch hour, when our guys on the street handed out the coupons, the capture ratio was amazing. Sales increased substantially, and the majority of the dollars dropped directly to the bottom line. That helped us meet some of our debt obligations and avoid layoffs over the long term. Once we regained our footing, we cut back the coupons and managed to maintain our price integrity without diminishing sales, despite the expectations and beliefs of the "experts."

From a sales point of view, our couponing campaign boosted the top line. And even more so, some of the reduced profit from the couponing discounts was offset by the savings we enjoyed from using skinless franks over the natural casings. However, if we didn't have anything on the top line, we wouldn't have *anything* trickling down to the bottom line. So couponing and skinless franks were equally critical to our recovery. But if I had to choose one or the other as the true game changer, couponing was likely the most important, "damage to the image" be damned.

While both initiatives helped stem the company's bleeding, we were far from out of the woods. In 1980, and with the company barely limping along, we shut down twenty-three restaurants in the metropolitan area alone, leaving only thirteen company-owned stores and ten franchises in the New York metro area. I was anxious and felt drained after all our hard work. I still worried how—or if— we were going to get through these challenges. How could I help? How could I ensure my young family's security? I realized I had a painful decision to make, but one that might help both my family and the company.

*Section 4*

# BUMPER CARS
# ON THE FREEWAY
## 1980's

## Chapter 7

# Margins and Marginality

*A*s much as I had been chomping at the bit to work full-time at Nathan's four years earlier, I now realized it might be time to leave my job. I told my father, "If you need me to leave and save the company money, I'll figure something out."

### My Sabbatical Year and Back: Arc of the Survivor

Regardless of his response, I knew it was time for me to leave. So I figured out a way to save the company money while remaining associated with and connected to Nathan's. I began speaking to a Nathan's franchise group about making a small investment to become part of their franchisee operations team. This offered an opportunity to develop Nathan's restaurants in Suffolk County on Long Island.

In addition, the group bought one of the existing Nathan's Famous corporate-owned stores at the Sunrise Mall in Massapequa. They offered me the opportunity to run it as a partner and general manager, with a salary and percentage interest in the total franchise group. It felt like a win-win-win situation for Nathan's, the franchise group, and me.

In 1980, Steve Winwood's album *Arc of a Diver* had just been released. I'd pop that cassette in the car tape deck every time I drove home from the late shift. Many of the tracks on that album spoke to what felt like a gut-wrenching situation, especially the ones titled "While You See a Chance [Take It]" and "Dust." I remember thinking, *Boy, did I see a chance and take it!*

Although I didn't know when, in the back of my mind I thought that someday I would return to Nathan's corporate headquarters. While I would have preferred to stay with the parent company, I had to do what was best for both my family and the company.

With the potential for success, the Suffolk franchise group seemed like a good opportunity. I enjoyed returning to the action, as I used to love it when I worked as a kid at the Coney Island and Oceanside locations. This opportunity brought me back to my first job. The realities of running a restaurant and everything it brings felt natural to me, especially once I implemented the previous lessons I learned from management experience at Nathan's corporate.

I enjoyed some good times as I settled in as GM. But the experience was not completely harmonious. I contended with the realities of frontline management duties and problems. The success or failure of a mall location hinges on its ability to capture its share of sales during peak periods of the year, so that it can survive during the slow times. That involves taking advantage of the crowds during busy season and doing everything humanly possible to bring in each potential dollar from the customers. Popular shopping times like Black Friday through New Year's Day weekend always presented a great opportunity to succeed. In fact, we'd take in 15 to 20 percent of our annual sales in just those five to six weeks. We had to run on all cylinders during that short period of time.

Unfortunately, even though we had the right product, the benefit of Nathan's brand, and a good location, we got financially strangled as a franchise group. One of our most significant issues was that we did not have a large enough customer base for our additional locations in Suffolk County to succeed.

Our success was considerably hindered when you combined the unfortunate timing of our financing with the lack of a customer base. Instead of putting up the money on our own, we borrowed it at a time when interest rates hit double digits. We were one of the many companies impacted by the deep recession that slammed economic activity and consumer spending in 1980-1981.

Our debt was prohibitive and became a heavy weight on our cash flow. I lost confidence in our ability to stay afloat, and I left after only fifteen months on the job, again sacrificing my position to try to save some money, and hoping the franchise group could hold on as long as it made sense. The franchise locations limped along for another year or so before finally closing.

Thankfully, I was able to return to Nathan's corporation as the director of corporate food service after my franchise stint ended in 1981. I was twenty-seven and eager to do whatever I could to improve the company. This position allowed me to work on the gamut of supermarket product development, restaurant product distribution, specifications, day-to-day problems, and everything to do with operations from the back-of-the-house perspective. I felt at home again! This time there was a new direction at the company with dramatic changes in restaurant management, concentration on all food and paper costs, as well reduced corporate overhead. Wayne, as head of operations, had been responsible for the development and implementation of these programs. I worked very closely with Wayne and all of the operations personnel to develop many food and paper goods specification changes that meant so much to the bottom line of the company over the next several years.

## Vendors Under Fire

As the director of corporate food service, I became intricately involved with managing operations, more so than ever before. This offered the opportunity to see many of the company's problems at close range and have the power to do something about it.

Much of my focus was on evaluating vendor relationships and streamlining our purchasing processes. There was still a top-to-bottom rift between the corporate staff, store management, and the operations team. Simultaneously, we had a huge problem with some dysfunctional vendors. I constantly heard about vendors delivering products late, not delivering food orders, and even bringing non-specified substitutes for those items that we ordered. For instance, if a paper supplier ran out of a certain paper good with the Nathan's logo, that vendor might try to slip in plain, non-logo items instead. This was totally unacceptable and occurred on a regular basis.

Managers also complained about the prices vendors offered, especially when they had contacts that could undercut them. I knew we could and should be getting better deals from our vendors. As I digested these problems, I reported them to my superior. I was dismayed that his reactions were slow.

> **Frank Lesson:** *As a leader, you have a responsibility to "turn over every stone" to ensure you are meeting the needs of the job.*

I believe the people in the department thought they had the best interests at heart for the company. However, they also thought they knew better than the people who worked in the stores. My predecessor in charge of purchasing was with the company for decades. He had two people supporting him: one who dealt with vendor deliveries to the stores and another who worked on product and service bids, sourcing, and everything else.

It didn't take long for me to understand that each store's management team could offer crucial input and feedback. They were the ones in the trenches. The purchasing department was not always in touch with the needs of the restaurant. I felt that the current process of evaluating our products and distribution methodology was not nearly as effective as it could be. Something had to change.

The department that developed the specifications for products the restaurants used or sold should invite, not dissuade, the restaurant staff to work through all the kinks before rolling out any new product, equipment, or operating process. We could have received important input had the purchasing department used operations personnel to thoroughly test a new item or process in a more cooperative environment.

After taking over the department, I was able to handle vendor problems with greater success. There were many basics that needed addressing, and I spent the majority of my time trying to correct them. I certainly appreciated the power and insight of the stores. Plus, I was even more motivated to make the company as efficient and profitable as possible during this tumultuous time. As the grandson of the founder and the son of the then current president and CEO, I felt the company—its past, present, and future—represented my legacy. So I took that position to heart and did all that I could.

Once I took the reins from my predecessor, I was on my own without any support staff. So I did the best I could, handling most of the day-to-day issues without assistance. At the time, I wondered if my father planned to let the vice president go so I could eventually take his position. Regardless, I put my head down and just focused on doing my job. Shortly thereafter, the vice president left and I was indeed promoted from director of corporate food service to his position as vice president of the same department.

With the new power this position provided, I started replacing vendors and manufacturers during the next couple of years. It was a tough transition involving difficult decisions, but I had no doubt that many of our old suppliers could not get the job done. While my father remained loyal to his longtime suppliers, he left me to make the important decisions of which ones to keep and which ones to change. I truly appreciated his confidence in my decisions, and I was determined to reward that trust by turning things around.

Generally speaking, the industry's "back-of-the-house" *modus operandi* was the fewer the suppliers the better, thereby allowing the restaurant to maintain a larger amount of control. However, we operated in the opposite way. We had many different distributors: for paper goods, potatoes, condiments, baked goods, and other products. Each of the many moving parts presented the opportunity for more problems. This was an old operating system concept.

One of our largest issues at the time was that we had two major hot dog manufacturers creating our product. There was also the issue of consistency. One manufacturer would deliver two good days of properly manufactured franks, then one day of fatty franks, which created an extensive amount of fat on the grill and did not meet our standards. This made it very difficult to operate the grill and caused us to serve an inferior product to our customers. Our store managers felt that the manufacturer was making up its margin on us. To us, it mattered little whether this was the result of purposeful behavior or simply quality control. Either way, the franks weren't good. The fact remained that we were receiving inferior product, which was completely unacceptable.

I had several discussions with Nathan's management regarding the benefit of maintaining two manufacturers. The response was that we needed two sources of supply to ensure we had some degree of leverage, and to protect ourselves in the event of any disaster that might befall one of the plants. So we sent a message to the underperforming vendor to stop screwing around. They needed to fix the problem, no matter what the cause. We built a business on serving a great product, and it started with quality of the hot dog. If they could not get the job done, we would just give our other vendor more frankfurter poundage production.

At the same time, I was looking to Morrell to satisfy our restaurant frankfurter needs, in addition to having them handle our supermarket-packaged program. This would help us accomplish two things. First, it would keep the local manufacturers in line with our needs. Second, from a marketing point of view, it would be beneficial to state that the same franks being sold in the restaurants were now also available in the supermarkets.

It was also important to evaluate those manufacturers and distributors utilized by the restaurants that weren't up to par. Some of these vendors serviced the company from my grandfather's early days, so I did my best to honor the relationships with those who were most loyal over the years. But it strained the operations. Most of the replaced vendors had older facilities and were falling behind. For example, one paper supplier was not using modern inventory control techniques, and its purchasing power was not nearly as great as that of its competitors.

I investigated and analyzed the entire distribution system, ushering in wholesale changes to ensure the back door would open just one-third of the time as it previously did. I also insisted vendors become more responsive to our restaurant managers' needs. My hope was that these changes would create a more efficient and streamlined approach to running our business.

Most, if not all, of the operations people respected these tough decisions. In their minds, these changes should have happened years ago. Some adjustments may seem almost trivial to an outsider, but they profoundly impacted the bottom-line daily operations.

We did more than just switch vendors. We also reevaluated what they supplied, which not only saved money but also helped us better serve our customers. A perfect example is how we replaced an eight-ounce cup with a boat tray for serving french fries. When he first opened the flagship Coney Island stand, my grandfather, Nathan, tried different style bags, from small wax bags to paper bags. The evolution of containers took us full circle from bags to cups to boat trays and back to bags again today only in Coney Island. The rest of the chain continues to use the boat trays.

From a food-cost point of view, cups limited the amount of fries an employee could give the customers, which enabled us to maintain consistent portions. However, the cups also detracted from perceived value and the customer's experience. That's because when customers squirted ketchup on fries in a cup, it only went on the top. What about the fries at the bottom? Customers would have to ask for another cup just for the ketchup. This added up, as each cup cost approximately two cents. Another problem was that cups filled with fries were so top heavy that, on countless occasions, customers would turn away from the counter only to have their cups topple over, spilling fries not just on the counter, but also on the floor.

I asked different paper suppliers for ideas. What's out there that can rectify this problem? We came up with a solution after talking with new vendors. It came in the form of boat trays, which were often used for BBQ chickens. We asked one supplier to make smaller boats for fries. The boat transformed the product by enhancing customers' perceived value and function, while cutting our costs and improving the operational impact to the company.

Instead of spending two cents for a cup and having customers use a second one just for ketchup, the small boat tray cost about a penny and solved both problems. Another advantage of the boat trays was that a case of one thousand was 30 percent smaller than one thousand cups, which reduced handling, packaging, and even storage space. The trays proved to be more efficient and less costly. Plus, customers would only require one boat tray because the fries could spread out, allowing ketchup to cover all of them. That practice enhanced the value to the customer because the boat tray carried more french fries. In fact, they overflowed, carrying more fries than the cups could contain. It was a homerun because the amount we saved on the boats exceeded the extra cost of offering customers a greater amount of fries per order.

But I knew we could do even better by controlling the amount of fries served in the boats. It took a bit of time to get this right. After repeatedly modifying the size of the boat tray, we finally found our sweet spot. At the time, and as a point of reference, McDonald's portions were 2.5 to 4 ounces, but their containers looked fuller than ours did. Because McDonald's fries are so thin, customers might think their servings appeared to have higher volume. However, they did not deliver on higher weight. Because of our adjustments, our portions gave both more volume and weight.

We figured that offering a 6 to 8 ounce tray overflowing with fries would not just create perceived value but would be more cost-effective and reduce lost product because of spills. To this day, the company uses these trays at most stores. This is one example of how seeing problems firsthand at the stores led to improvements on many dimensions.

> **Frank Lesson:** *Even a small adjustment can create great results.*

Around this time my father worked hard to oversee strategies to remain in business. That included continuing to divest the remaining failed Wetson's stores Nathan's had acquired five years prior. Additionally, management targeted both chain operators and individual owners as potential buyers.

We barely limped along even with all these advancements. That is until serendipity brought about a very positive occurrence: the Marriott Corporation inquired about available Nathan's restaurant locations for sale.

## Marriott: Saving Grace

In 1980, Marriott was expanding the Roy Rogers restaurant chain it owned. It was looking to use the new fast food chain to take the New York market by storm.

This sparked many possible solutions. One option was to offer the whole company up for sale. If Marriott held our feet to the fire, it probably could have bought the entire company for $2 million, or thereabouts. But Marriott only wanted restaurant locations that it felt could provide the best exposure in the New York marketplace for Roy Rogers. It didn't want to become distracted from its corporate goals by dealing with another fast food company that had a very different concept, no matter how much value or potential upside it represented.

In the fall of 1980, Marriott purchased seven Nathan's stores for the same $2 million that we might have accepted for the entire company. That pivotal sale saved Nathan's Famous from bankruptcy.

Murray, who had assigned Harold Norbitz to help spearhead the contract negotiation for licensing to supermarkets, also proved to be very helpful during the Marriott contract discussions. The deal for these stores was the catalyst for the next stage in the developmental process of the company. In fact, we could not concentrate on further growth paths without the cash from the sale of the stores.

Call it luck, call it tremendous negotiations, call it Murray's guidance and faith, or call it the complete dedication of the Nathan's staff to make this company survive and see it grow to the status it deserved. Whatever you want to call it, I believe it was all of the above, not just one of these independent factors that enabled us to move forward.

Although we were now able to pay off our debt and stuff our coffers with some cash, we still had to figure out the best strategic direction for the company. Not surprising, there was significant disagreement among top management. This time the integral issue was regarding the testing of new store concepts and locations. There was no doubt that we should test new restaurants under the Nathan's brand name—the question was how and where?

## Testing Where to Go from Here

With this new effort, our challenge involved testing the opportunities with the most potential. Where were the prospects? What were the risks? What were the potential rewards? We had to identify one or more restaurant prototypes that we could adapt to numerous situations for both company-owned stores and potential new franchisees.

Management did agree on our main objective: pare down the menu to its essence, which consisted of hot dogs, fries, and whatever other items might fit into the local market's unique tastes. Individual stores retained the ability to expand or contract the menu according to the local marketing opportunities.

We made decisions on menu items not just based on profit margin. If a particular item produced low margins but higher volume and net dollars, we might keep it on the menu because of its overall dollar profit contribution to the bottom line. On the other hand, we might decide to drop a high-margin but low-volume menu item because it would be hard to preserve the freshness of a product due to sporadic sales.

Another consideration was the impact of cutting out a bunch of items that would have been on a store's menu for "variety." We had sold potato knishes for years, but we decided to eliminate them from the menu because they were taking sales away from french fries and they were not as profitable. We were certain we still had a varied menu without knishes. To find the right balance, I worked with managers and supervisors on a store-by-store basis to determine the best locations for these items.

The beauty of the Nathan's Famous concept was that we could provide a full menu in freestanding stores and pared-down menus in the smaller, captive-market situations like stadiums, highway rest stops, and malls. One item we usually could not offer in most malls was hamburgers, because of competition from existing restaurant chains in the food courts. However, we did have our own hamburger menu and included it wherever we were permitted to sell the product line.

> **Frank Lesson:** *Know your brand and understand your business. An intricate and intimate knowledge of who you are can often keep you afloat.*

As we started to test the waters, my main focus was to help the operations department develop menus and specification systems for each item and each prototype. Based on the success of many food toppings, we added several options to all existing stores. Toppings such as crushed bacon, chili, cheese sauce, and baked beans provided us with higher sales and profits without great equipment expense or operational difficulty.

Still, management couldn't agree with one another about where to test our new concepts. Some of us insisted that we test different prototypes in our prime, captive-market sites to learn which ones would receive the most acceptance. This camp favored controlled areas such as mall food courts that would not be as expensive to construct as new in-line or freestanding locations.

Others felt that we should mainly focus our tests in our hometown of New York. The thinking here was that we should seize every opportunity to capture a good location and take advantage of our strong name recognition and reputation.

In the end, we decided to test the concepts inside and outside of New York. We invested almost $1 million, which included some proceeds from the Marriott deal and some cash flow from existing profitable stores.

We opened our first test restaurant outside of New York at one of the largest malls on the East Coast, The King of Prussia Mall in Pennsylvania. There, we implemented a very limited menu in a high-volume mall. We conducted our second test at the Latham Circle Mall in upstate New York, outside of Albany. These stores were small units, about five hundred to six hundred square feet. For our first test in the metro area, we built a larger in-line store in midtown Manhattan, which included a full menu, with breakfast offerings and a dining room area.

We worked with our architect, and our team in operations to come up with methodology and equipment to install in the test stores. We had to figure out how the test locations were going to heat food. Our old stores had stoves for heating sauerkraut in a double-pot boiler, but the new and smaller stores had no room to house a stove. Although microwaves for reheating food were already an industry standard, we had no need for them until we began testing new store concepts and toppings.

We decided that across the board microwaves were the most time-efficient and cost-effective way to heat up food such as soups, sauerkraut, and other toppings. Eliminating stoves in all of our stores would save room, time, and expensive gas bills. We developed operationally efficient procedures for handling the new products' storage, preparation, and service.

We continued to tinker with the product and the process. While we were busy making changes to our offerings for the prototypes, I also worked on adjusting our entire distribution systems and product packaging. The use of a single "master distributor" was critical to our national growth. We worked to devise a combination of goods that could be shipped around the country with enough unit volume to work for both end-user restaurants as well as the distributor. Thus, we had to minimize the number of Nathan's proprietary goods that did not create enough weekly movement. Any distributor would find it problematic to hold proprietary goods lacking enough weekly movement. This impacted stores that could not generate substantial turnover or lacked significant storage space.

Over the next few years, our tests in and out of New York failed. The prototypes proved to be marginal at best, but already successful existing stores like Yonkers, Oceanside, and some of the remaining converted Wetson's locations enjoyed the positive distribution and product modification changes.

However, throughout the prototype testing process we did learn a lot, especially that there was not enough profit to be squeezed in the structure of company-owned locations outside the New York market. The problem was supervision. Each store required a manager on Nathan's corporate payroll, as well as a supervisor's time for in-store visits. Most company-owned prototype stores didn't generate enough sales to offset these costs. We also learned that certain prototype stores could be profitable for a "mom and pop" franchise run by owners who don't need to pay themselves a large salary. They could oversee their store themselves without the layer of a paid general manager/supervisor, while living off the store's profits.

Based on all that we learned, with great success we switched our strategy to institute limited renovations at company-owned legacy stores. Still, there were no homeruns in or outside of New York. Even our large investment in an in-line, midtown store just did not produce enough profits to justify the costs. We ultimately closed it.

## Searching for New Blood

During this period, with all the transactions and ongoing tests, I loved my work and felt committed to helping the company move forward. And we *were* moving forward, however cautiously.

I knew that without the Marriott deal, we might have had to declare bankruptcy. My father's perseverance, along with our relationships with all the vendors, helped us survive those dark days. His belief in our company and the dedication of our employees to keep the business going was undeniable. However, Murray was tiring. The company's downturn, especially the struggle to dig the company out of debt, took its toll on him. Once we were back on solid footing, my mother wanted him out of the company and at home in a less tense setting.

*These were some of the longtime employees at Coney Island (ranging from 1936 to 1979). Pictured: (L-R) Sing King Lo (Sinta), Ernest Benson, Murray Handwerker, John Pao, Thomas Settle, and Willie Robbins at Pao's 1979 retirement party*
*Photo Credit: Bill Mitchell Photography*

## Chapter 8

# Nathan's Goes Private Again

**B**y 1983, we were able to dig out of debt after all our efforts to cut costs, improve the top and bottom lines, and thanks to the remarkable events that transpired at the eleventh hour with the white knight Marriott. But Murray, now sixty-two, was exhausted and stressed to the max. Since he was fifty-five, my mother had been after him to retire. Over the years, she told me several times she felt he had done his time and put his sweat and blood into the family business. It was also apparent to her, to me, and finally to my father that Nathan's Famous needed a new direction and a new generation of leadership. But, unfortunately, Murray's determination to find top talent from outside the company further divided existing management.

### Flagging Confidence in Management

Many of us felt insiders were more than qualified to take the company to the next level. But not everyone felt that way. Perhaps it was this squabbling that distracted us, creating mediocre results at best, even after all our hard-earned progress. Initially I felt that we could succeed with inside management and expressed that feeling to Murray. But rather than trying to get my father to agree, and rather than initiating an executive search, I began to hunt for a consultant who could analyze our situation and advise Murray on our next steps, with the same vision I had for the company's future leadership.

My father did not believe that existing management could make his dreams come true because he felt that expansion required a more experienced leader. Another factor was his trust and faith in outside consultants.

Remember that in the early days, Murray had almost singlehandedly accomplished major expansions, first with the menu in the early 1950s, then by opening new locations from the mid-1950s through the 1970s, and finally with the licensing program. Even before Nathan passed the torch to his son, Murray was both the mastermind and executor when it came to strategy. My father did not micromanage or hover over his team, at least when it came to tactics.

With the addition of the Times Square location, this management style led to some expansion problems. For example, Murray's lieutenants completely overbuilt and over budgeted the original Times Square store's construction, which was a big drag on the company until it closed in the early 1990s. Even with those problems, the Coney Island, Oceanside, and Yonkers locations remained extremely profitable. In fact, when there was good weather in Coney Island during the summer, this location produced an unbelievably disproportionate amount of the company's sales and profit, at least until the licensing program took off.

But as the company began to find places in Nathan's executive suite for several of Wetson's managers like the Norbitzes, it became clear that they wanted to follow their own ideas about strategy and tactics. Murray mostly stood back and let the Norbitzes do their job. In fact, both Wayne and Harold proved themselves to be very effective: Harold with franchising, real estate, and various company contract negotiations, and Wayne with restaurant operations.

But after suffering through and emerging from enormous economic threats and pressures, Murray, though drained, was itching to move forward with further expansion. Wayne, Ken, the operations team, and I were ready to go. But my father remained unsatisfied with the current makeup of management and still wanted to look outside of the company, a tendency he often fell back on.

He believed that we required new blood with some combination of experience in large restaurant operations, franchising, and the ability to expand initiatives exponentially.

Wayne and I disagreed with his assessment. In fact, we were upset about Murray's position, which disheartened existing management. Despite the fact that we just successfully ushered the company through difficult times, Murray was certain that we would have failed but for the Marriott deal. There may have been truth to that, but the opposite was also true. The company would have failed had it not been for the determination, expertise, and shrewdness of management, even with the Marriott deal. In spite of this, Murray insisted that the company needed a new direction and new blood.

## Outsiders Step In

With the writing on the wall, I wanted to make sure I had some input on Murray's choice of hiring an outside executive. My objective was to find a consultant who could sift through our situation and advise my father that current management could successfully run the business and that we did not have a permanent need for anyone from the outside. We simply had to figure out how to find a direction that everyone could live with and then productively move forward.

I was confident that choosing the right outside consultant could show Murray we had what it took to get us to the next level so long as we could experiment and evaluate results along the way to see which concepts would let us accomplish the vision we were destined to attain.

I found and then recommended that we bring in Bob Rosenthal, the Chairman and CEO with First Long Island Investor's (FLI) a financial services company. He spent more than ten years at Entenmann's Inc., most recently as executive vice president and chief operating officer. Entenmann's, the very successful family-owned baked goods company, was one of the best examples of what a family-run company could accomplish. They created a quality product line surviving different operating opinions and were thriving. Bob was always professional, always pleasant, and always formal. He joined us along with his two associates, Ralph Palleschi and George Rifkin, who also had been executives at Entenmann's.

I met Bob at a social event months before introducing him to Murray. I asked him to test some Entenmann's desserts in a half dozen of our stores. We had unsuccessfully tried many different dessert approaches in the past and thought this change might do the trick. But we yawned at the results. We didn't blame Entenmann's product line for the shortcomings. Generally, the fast food industry doesn't do well with dessert sales. Slow sales produce extensive waste from the high proportion of leftovers and outdated products. Another problem was that Entenmann's offerings were too costly for our fast food menu. However, because other fast food restaurants offered desserts, we felt it was important to keep similar (but more moderately priced) confections on our menu.

I was impressed with him and his team, even though the dessert test failed. Especially welcoming was their ability to work successfully with Entenmann's co-owners (multiple siblings) over the course of many years. This experience convinced me that he would be a good fit for Nathan's. In my mind, that was justification enough to suggest that I invite Bob to meet Murray.

My father and I felt that some of the parallels between Entenmann's and Nathan's would enable Rosenthal to understand and appreciate our company. Like Nathan's, Entenmann's maintained a deep multigenerational history and a brand-name product with tremendous growth possibilities. Bob agreed and indicated he always thought that the Nathan's brand had similar potential.

I believed Bob would be able to work effectively with me and the rest of management, bring us together, and help us develop our future plans, while simultaneously respecting Murray's ultimate objective. I hoped we could accomplish my agenda of keeping the team in place and that this time in our company's history a consulting arrangement would help us find solutions to our problems and opportunities without a management change.

After a few meetings, my father agreed to hire Bob's company to develop a five-year plan with management. They also met extensively with Nathan's executives and developed an opinion of staff functions and leadership. Palleschi and Rifkin did most of the legwork inside our company, while Rosenthal handled oversight and led the analysis of their findings.

In the process, Bob developed a trusted relationship with Murray and Dorothy. He gave them the respect they were due, but would not hesitate to tell them things they might not want to hear. My mistake was thinking that Bob would view Nathan's future direction the same way I did.

## The New Five-Year Plan

Both First Long Island Investors and company management rejected the idea of expanding geographically after multiple sit-down meetings to develop the five-year plan, because our previous tests outside New York were unsuccessful. Murray's main concern at that point was to secure his and the company's futures. We would likely have to turn to alternative opportunities if we did not open more corporate stores, and if existing franchisees were producing mixed results under the current operating structure.

The one thing we agreed upon was the need to renovate many of our current locations. We began to consider the amount of money the company should commit to this effort. In particular, four stores were prime candidates for this project: Yonkers, Oceanside, 86th Street in Brooklyn, and Kings Plaza Mall in Brooklyn. They all were old and needed updating. Our operations people knew the investment would pay heavy dividends if we upgraded the stores. Murray was receptive but also apprehensive about investing huge sums of money because Nathan's Famous had only recently secured stronger footing. At that point in his life, he was only willing to commit dollars from cash flow and refused to take on debt with its inherent risk, especially in the event that the renovations did not produce positive outcomes.

Wayne prepared a presentation to the board that featured a five-year projection of the results the renovations might produce. He outlined a budget with expected sales and profit. His estimates projected substantial returns. On all levels, Wayne worked to implement an improved system of operating, focusing on "wowing" the customer by exceeding their expectations. With Murray's approval, Wayne and the operations team also created a new incentive plan that helped motivate managers to meet their sales and profit objectives.

The renovation program was a huge success, thanks largely to the hard work of a support staff that believed in and implemented the plan. The updated store environment instilled a new pride among the store management. In addition, we retrained the store operating staff using typical industry programs while restaurant management trained the line staff to provide a new level of attention to customers, which would ensure their increased satisfaction.

We constantly evaluated results, from a profit-and-loss (P&L) perspective, and tracked how customers perceived their dining experience. Sales and profits followed after our commitment to make the customer our top priority. Finally, our culture and morale were in sync, pushing the company forward.

Still, I felt we had to change one major menu issue: returning to the natural casing and stop selling skinless hot dogs (at the restaurants, but not at the supermarkets). Many others in the company agreed. To help us survive during the late 1970s and throughout the early 1980s, we sold the higher-margin skinless dogs at our restaurants (except in Coney Island). While the skinless franks were definitively accepted by our customers and maintained the highest quality possible, everyone at the company knew that the skinless frank deviated from the one that made Nathan's famous.

Along with Ken, Wayne, and the majority of the team, I felt that in the long term, an original Nathan's Famous natural casing frank was the best marketing tool we could use to increase sales and entice new franchisees to buy into the Nathan's system. But we still had the issue of cost and profit. So when we returned to the lower-margin natural casing frank, we decided to increase pricing over time to negate the hit to the bottom line. Luckily, we experienced no negative effect on sales from the nominal price increase.

We could no longer ignore the unresolved issue of future leadership once we began executing the five-year plan. Murray was eager to retire, and we had to figure out who would lead the company in the future.

## Figuring Out New Leadership

My father and the FLI team were uncertain that neither Wayne nor I were ready for the top leadership role, even after our five-year plan's strategies and tactics began producing positive results. There was no problem with our performance. They just felt that the company needed a leader who had the experience to take us to the next level.

However, to my surprise, I was called to meet with my father and Bob. Murray asked me if I wanted the position of executive vice president, to potentially be groomed to become president in the future. Bob said that he would remain as our consultant and work with me for as long as needed. I recall that my father acted like he didn't really want to offer me this shot and harbored mixed feelings. Despite his desire for a more seasoned leader with larger-company experience, on some level he wanted the company and its legacy to continue as a family business, with a Handwerker in charge. But would Murray really have gone through with his invitation? I don't know. It would have required at least two years of his guidance just to get me settled into the job, which my mother would never have tolerated.

I was tempted to accept my father's offer, but I hesitated and did not jump on the offer. I asked myself, "Do I really want to do this?" With all my experience at the corporate and store levels, I knew I could do the job. But the timing was wrong for me, as my family had just experienced a crisis that motivated me to want to maintain a healthy work-home balance.

As John Lennon said, "Life happens when you are busy making other plans." A year or so prior to this discussion, my younger son Michael, just two years old, almost died from a serious allergic reaction to an inoculation. His airway was closing and he would have stopped breathing if he had not gotten to the emergency room ASAP. If it weren't for the quick thinking of my wife, Amy, and our doctor, Michael wouldn't have survived. I felt helpless while his life was hanging in the balance. As a result, I shifted to making decisions based on the things I *could* control.

Because I grew up without my father available to throw a ball around with me, I told Amy I didn't want to do the same thing with our kids. I wanted to make time to coach my sons, take them to ballgames, go to the many different events that happen during their young lives, and just be present when they had the need for me to listen, especially after almost losing Michael.

I understand that many people feel they have no choice but to work long and hard to get ahead professionally and financially. In fact, many people would have jumped at the offer, even if it was really not genuine, to be groomed for the eventual presidency. However, I came to the realization that this was just not the right choice for me. My priorities had changed.

I was still an emotional wreck even a year after my son's near-death experience. My mind constantly raced at a million miles an hour. I not only needed but wanted lots of time for my family. Taking the reins would have compromised my resolve to maintain a work-life balance. So I suggested that Wayne take the executive vice president position, while I became second in command. Since Wayne first came to the company, I worked well with him and expected to continue doing so in the future. We shared a consistent vision for the company.

After I filled Wayne in on my meeting, I asked him what he thought about my response to Murray's offer. He replied, "Do you really think that would happen? Don't you think Murray would prefer to sell the company if the continuity of Handwerker management wasn't present?" He was correct.

*William Handwerker and Family -1988*
*First row (L-R) Adam and Michael; second row (L-R) William, Amy*
*Photo Credit: Bill Mitchell Photography*

Did my father really think Wayne and I couldn't do the job together? I believe that Murray had mixed feelings about Harold and Wayne. Deep down, I'm sure that Murray recognized they were effective leaders and, more important, that they had Nathan's best interest at heart.

During a recent conversation with Bob, I inquired as to why he and Murray rejected Wayne as the future company leader, especially considering that Wayne was successful in the roles of President and COO at Nathan's Famous since 1990 before retiring in 2015. Rosenthal told me that back then, Wayne just wasn't ready, and that Murray would not put the future of Nathan's in his hands.

To whatever extent that may be true, I'm sure my father worried about how to extricate himself from the company in a way that would secure his own financial future as well as that of his siblings. He knew that once he left, his B shares would have to be liquidated. Because the B shares held all the voting rights, selling his stake would change the balance of power, making it difficult for any future leader to control the company in the way my father did. According to the company's bylaws, Murray was not permitted to sell or gift his shares to anyone. Another concern was that if Murray were to retire and sell the company, then some family members who owned stock but did not work at the company would have to be made whole in some fashion.

If I had lobbied strongly to keep the company in the family, and if I had taken the executive vice president position to make that happen, it would not have been an easy transition. Later, Wayne asked me, "Do you really think the board and your father would have eventually made you president if Murray had left?" Well, we'll never know the answer to that question.

Bob told me that he would have loved for me to become president. He believes the board would have approved it and continued retaining his services. Upon reflection, the main issue was how long Murray was willing to stay at the helm to create this scenario, and I knew it wasn't going to be for long.

At the time, and after considering all my options, I ended up telling my father, "You have to do what's best for you. Don't worry about me; I'll take care of myself." That's when I decided definitively that the executive vice president position was not for me. But I was confident the company would maintain my then current position at least for a few years because I knew my job, and they would need me, no matter who ended up in charge. The company did keep me on for nine more years through the eventual sale and several subsequent transitions of outside leadership.

To fill our management vacuum, the company hired an executive search firm to find leaders from outside our company with franchising and/or family business experience. I was not part of the search until near the end of the process when, in 1985, we hired George Haggerty as Nathan's executive vice president in charge of franchised stores.

George was previously a top executive of Dunkin' Donuts Inc. He later went on to become the head of Hair Club for Men. Despite some previous accomplishments, he turned out to be an unfortunate choice because his contributions did not result in a significant improvement over existing management's direction or bottom-line results.

In November 1986 a corporate profile in the now-defunct magazine *Manhattan Inc.* quoted the even-tempered, affable George Haggerty as saying he initially questioned whether or not he "really want[ed] to get messed up in this," referring to Nathan's. At the time, he felt our operations were unlike the modern cookie-cutter stores and tight-run ships he was used to. He was also concerned about working at a family operation where five of the six top executives were either from the Handwerker or Norbitz families, some of whom he sensed didn't get along and may not have wanted an outsider running the company.

But George was impressed with how Nathan's had extricated itself from its mid- to late-1970s crises by slicing overhead and ditching under-performing locations. He also seemed to respect Murray's determination to learn from past mistakes, which Murray described in the same *Manhattan Inc.* article: "What I realized after I closed so many stores was that in the future, I was going to have to depend on people who really know what was going on in the fast food industry, and not these accountants and lawyers with their figures and pieces of paper."

So George accepted our offer, lured by Murray's vision of expansion and desire to find high-powered talent with a battle plan for implementing the company's strategic goals. First and foremost, these included further streamlining the company. He was in charge of developing action plans, budgets, as well as training and locating a real estate selection company. He also recognized the need for unifying inside managers. After his first department-head meeting, he claimed that the head of personnel told him that was the first time in five years that they had all sat down at the same table. "I forced people to work together who weren't used to working together," he told the magazine.

I imagine that my grandfather, Nathan, turned in his grave at the prospect of having an outsider run his company. I shared his skepticism. Despite George's credentials and background with franchising, he ended up doing little to develop our new restaurants and the franchise program for whatever reasons that could be attributed. He couldn't meet the needed expansion goal.

As a result, just over a year after the decision to bring in outside management, Murray and the board no longer considered George a viable candidate for the top spot. Once again, with no designated successor to Murray, a feeling of limbo began to sink in among Wayne, others in management, and myself. The choice seemed obvious to some: sell the company. I disagreed, but the stars were not aligned to keep the company in current management's hands, and Murray didn't want to take any more chances.

He was looking for a permanent solution and felt the company was on solid financial footing and well poised to sell at a good price. He was correct, although we did have to deal with a few sobering false starts.

## On the Block

Murray insisted that any buyer we chose maintain the ability to take Nathan's to the next level. This would require a purchaser with a proven track record of helping or developing other companies' national expansions. He also wanted to secure the Nathan's experience for future generations of consumers. Any serious bidder would have to understand the Nathan's brand, business model, culture, and exactly what keeps loyal customers coming back.

Initially Nathan's approached Pepsi (which owned several fast food restaurant chains) and other national firms to buy the company. We would have loved to approach Coca-Cola, our longtime partner, but they were not in or interested in entering the restaurant business. As hard as we tried to pitch our proposition to the big boys, those potential suitors rejected the idea. They felt we were primarily New York centric, without a major presence throughout

*Nathan's Times Square 1986,
Murray Handwerker and
Mayor Edward Koch at the
70th anniversary party.*

*70ᵗʰ anniversary celebration crowd looking at
Murray and Mayor Ed Koch during the celebration.
Photo Credit: Bill Mitchell Photography for both photos*

the rest of the country. They also felt we were too small. They didn't see our potential for expansion. I understand their perspective, especially because our test prototypes, such as those in King of Prussia, Pennsylvania, and Latham, New York, produced marginal results.

Another problem was that we were a hybrid food company with two main revenue streams: the restaurants and selling packaged product by the pound to supermarkets and other outlets. Perhaps our licensee, Morrell, would have made a logical suitor, at least for us, but not for them. Morrell had a huge contract with us, and that revenue source eventually doubled our bottom line. Why would Morrell want to buy us when it was already controlling the product now in the supermarket trade without the headache of learning how to actually manage our restaurants? They enjoyed much of the positive with little of the negative.

We had to clearly reset our sights by approaching potential acquirers who were smaller or local, perhaps like a venture capital group. Two suitors emerged. The first prospective buyer was one of the largest restaurant real estate owners in New York at the time, with many prime locations throughout the city. But in November 1986, they quickly dropped out of the bid with a lowball offer of $16 million.

A second opportunity surfaced later that month from Richard and Steven Buckley, wealthy Long Island business owners who had created Equicor Group Limited, a private investment company looking to acquire companies in the food industry. They were the two people who would be the operators, if successful in the bid, and represented a group of seven limited partnerships that would provide the money for any deal to be consummated.

In early 1987, Equicor offered $7.50 per share (while Nathan's 2.25 million common shares were trading for $6.625 per share), which came to about $17 million. After Nathan's board quickly charged its financial advisors (Oppenheimer & Company and First Long Island Investors) to study the chain's alternatives, Murray and the board rejected that offer. Murray told the press at the time that it was his responsibility "to maximize value to the stockholders, including myself." Ultimately the investors upped their bid to $8.50 per share, which came to a little more than $19 million.

Even with that bid on the table, other issues almost derailed the deal. Murray was not happy with how things were proceeding at that time and something had change. My father brought in Howard Lorber, one of the lead partners in one of the seven limited partnerships, to consummate the deal. He told me the next day that we never would have been able to close the deal if it hadn't been for Lorber taking over for the Buckleys and pulling everyone together.

Perhaps it should have come as no surprise that the Equicor merger was not a marriage made in heaven.

# VIEW FROM
# THE FERRIS WHEEL
## 1990's – Present

*Photo Credit: Wonder Wheel – Deno Vourderis*

## Chapter 9

# Private Again, Public Again

*T*he deal closed in 1987, and the new owners from Equicor offered me a three-year contract the moment the ink dried on the letter of agreement to sell Nathan's. I ended up staying on until 1996, for nine years after the sale. Even though my VP of corporate food service title did not change, everything else seemed to, especially after my father retired, and then again three years later when my brother Kenny exited the company.

It was very strange to walk into my father's old office and not see him behind his desk. We'd no longer be able to sit and have talks during his lunch, which he usually brought from home. I was the only Handwerker left to carry on the family tradition after Ken departed. I had a small empty feeling inside. Maybe this was a warning of things to come for me as well. Those thoughts didn't usually last long, but in the back of my mind I often wondered, when would my days at Nathan's end, and how?

With my father's controlling stake liquidated, the company was no longer in my family's control. As a result, I was no longer involved in high-level discussions about strategy or operations. Intellectually, I understood why, but emotionally

I had some expectation that management would include or even consult with me in decisions about company direction. I was now just an employee, who happened to be a part of the founding family, which didn't seem to count for much under the new regime.

Despite my new status in the company, I was still able to express my opinions about anything to do with our restaurant menu, service methodology, supermarket products, manufacturing, and distribution. Equicor's Richard and Steven Buckley—Nathan's chairman and executive vice president/chief operating officer respectively—listened when I had something to say about those issues.

Wayne and I agreed on most, if not all, operating procedures. Mostly, I was content to focus on my job and work as hard as ever, but without as much pressure now that I was out of the loop of corporate-level decision making. I no longer had any exposure or input to the inner thinking of upper management on the future direction of the company or even day to day issues if it didn't have to do with my work purview. This was a new world that I had to get used to.

## New Regimes

The Buckley brothers wasted no time wiping out most remnants of the old guard. The most poignant instance was when I walked past a service elevator outside our office and found they had dumped a pile of framed paintings, photos, letters, and other mementos from as far back as my grandfather's reign. They had stacked precious emblems from our company's heritage and culture that used to hang throughout the offices in and all around the large, overflowing trash bin. Among the tossed items were:

- Pictures of my father with Mayor Koch on our 70th anniversary
- Letters from former New York City mayors Abe Beam, Ed Koch, and John Lindsay, plus New York State Senate members, mostly thanking us for helping with various donations
- Caricatures of my father and grandfather by famed *New York Post* artist, the late John Pierotti (with a caption identifying my grandfather announcing Roadside Rest in Oceanside); another one with both my dad and grandfather wearing bowties.

- A 1970 caricature of Murray on a hot dog roll by David Levine, one of the premier caricaturists in the world, best known for his cartoons in the *New York Review of Books,* whose work has also appeared in major art exhibits.

The only mementos the Buckleys kept were the original griddle and a couple of gallon jugs that used to sit on top of ceramic bases to dispense the grape, pineapple, and orange drinks.

I couldn't understand what they were doing. When I asked them why they were dumping the company's history, they responded: "Well, we want to change the whole approach." So I asked, "Can I have the memorabilia?" When they said yes, I salvaged many of these items, which now grace the walls of my home. Still shaken, I relayed this egregious snub to my father and family. Murray agreed that the Buckleys obviously had no sense of tradition, but he seemed more dismissive about the issue than I was.

Looking back, perhaps losing important parts of our culture with that transition was not as monumental as I made it out to be—at least not in the grand scheme of things. But I still feel some disbelief and outrage. Their perception of trash was part of a bigger problem: they ignored the company's rich and proud culture that my grandfather and father built.

On the positive side, the Buckleys offered to let me use my father's old desk. It was made from oak with green leather top inserts and gold braided trim. I happily accepted and moved it to my office, replacing the standard office's fake wood top and steel-drawer desk. This proved to be the only physical reminder of my father and his legacy that remained in the corporate office. I appreciated being able to sit at the same desk as my father for the years I remained at Nathan's. The company offered to let me keep it when I left, but the other mementos I recovered from the garbage seemed much more important tokens of my memories and family's legacy.

Most of the people who came with the Wetson's acquisition exhibited more respect for the past, especially when it came to my father and grandfather. Although it would make sense to continue to mention the founder in marketing campaigns, there was minimal reference to Nathan—let alone Murray at all.

At some point, the thought to take advantage of the heritage did occur to management. We selected Lou Jacoby to portray Nathan Handwerker in a series of commercials. Jacoby was the actor who played the Dunkin' Donuts baker and uttered the famous words "Time to make the donuts," as well as the Breakstone Dairy man in a series of commercials. I worked on the commercials to ensure that the food they displayed appeared appetizing. However, to my knowledge these commercials never aired. I don't know why we did not pursue this or any television advertising campaigns, even after those commercials were produced.

While Equicor's limited partners were mostly accountants, insurance executives, pension practitioners, businessmen, and attorneys, the Buckleys did have some experience in the food industry, as they previously operated a large catering operation. But that's not the same as the fast food business. I was about to learn how to operate under new management, just as they were about to hop onto a steep learning curve regarding our industry and company.

The Buckleys signed up a restaurant franchise/real estate company as a major franchisee in 1988, which opened a dozen Nathan's units in Manhattan. Interestingly enough, this franchisee happened to be the company that had earlier competed with Equicor and made the lowball offer to purchase Nathan's.

Meanwhile, despite some progress under the Buckleys' leadership with franchising and our retail/licensing program, Nathan's other programs remained status quo. Just two years after we sold Nathan's, some of Equicor's limited partners quickly became disenchanted with the Buckley brothers' lack of expansion growth.

## The New World Order

In March 1989, Richard and Steven Buckley resigned from the company and sold their interest to two other Equicor limited partners: Stuart Benson and William Landsberg. Benson, who was functioning as chairman of the executive committee, then helped to form a new partnership, Benson/Landsberg Associates, which specialized in corporate acquisitions and real estate. They teamed with Anfang Resources Inc. Benson became Nathan's chairman, while William Landsberg and Stephen Anfang became vice chairmen.

The new owners and top management seemed to get off to a good start. They installed Robert J. Sherman, an alumnus of Prudential-Bache Securities' retail group, as president and CEO. "I know how to build a staff and support expansion—that's the most important thing," Sherman told the press at the time. He certainly had a good track record, previously directing a large expansion for Prudential-Bache from 1982-1988, from 100 offices and 2,100 brokers to 275 offices and 5,100 brokers.

Together, the new owners and management team aggressively slashed expenses, implementing actions such as moving headquarters from the pricey midtown Manhattan location to the Long Island town of Westbury. I am not sure how much money the company saved by making the move, but we spent a lot of money on the design of the offices, including a test kitchen, which seemed unnecessary to me because we had a perfectly good kitchen ten minutes from the Westbury office, at our Hicksville store.

When the company was sold, I found it ironic that we moved from New York City to Long Island because one of the main reasons Murray moved the company headquarters from Brooklyn to Manhattan was to obtain additional exposure to potential franchise investors. The new owners felt a New York City presence was unnecessary for promoting the business. My father remained unfazed when he learned of the move.

Despite my doubts regarding the benefits to the company, I was extremely happy to avoid the daily commute to the city and replace it with a relatively easy fifteen- to twenty-minute drive from my Long Island home. To save money, we sublet some of the space we didn't need, including the test kitchen. We made the move from the city, but I always wondered what we lost in marketing exposure.

The new management's efforts to expand were also ambitious. By the end of the year, they planned to open forty-five company-owned and franchised Nathan's restaurants from coast to coast in airport terminals, highway rest stops, and shopping malls. The Marriott Corporation, which purchased Nathan's units several years before, returned with plans to operate new Nathan's restaurants on major highway rest stops in Florida and Massachusetts. The smaller Nathan's stores would concentrate on hot dogs and fries, while the larger stores would also sell sandwiches, seafood, chicken, hamburgers, and other items.

We received incredible publicity when we opened a new company store in Chicago. The doors hadn't even opened and the buzz was significant. While I was in town setting up the store, one local newspaper published an article titled "Big Apple, Windy City Relish War of the Dogs"[13] that stated we should stay in New York, and that Chicago didn't need another hot dog. It was either written tongue-in-cheek or the city had a real ego problem. The fact was, we knew that Chicagoans were major consumers of frankfurters, and we were just trying to make a buck—not go to war with Chicago's other eateries.

Initially I thought it was hilarious that we appeared in the newspapers this way. But the store closed just a few months after it opened. I believe the reason we did not succeed in this endeavor is because we chose the wrong neighborhood location. I still feel Chicago would have welcomed Nathan's with open arms if we had chosen the right location.

Even if the time I spent on the store was unsuccessful, I had a unique opportunity on this weekend trip to Chicago to be with my oldest son, Adam. I took him with me without Amy or Michael. I wanted him to have a little special "alone time" with his dad. I really enjoyed the time we spent together. He did his homework during the day sitting at a table in the restaurant while I was working. He got to see me at work and enjoyed that. At night we went to dinner. This was the first time either of us had tried "Chicago Deep Dish Pizza." Neither of us liked the pizza, it was so heavy! Even so, our time together was great. It was the best part of my work in that town.

The new Benson/Landsberg/Stuart and Sherman administration ushered in rewarding and exciting times for me personally at the company. One highlight was when the new leadership team sent me halfway around the world to set up vendors for the opening of new stores.

---

13  "Big Apple, Windy City Relish War of the Dogs" by Mario Fox, Associated Press writer Published: Sunday, Feb. 11 1990 http://www.deseretnews.com/article/86159/BIG-APPLE-WINDY-CITY-RELISH-WAR-OF-THE-DOGS.html?pg=all (accessed Jan. 8, 2015).

## Taking Nathan's to Russia

I truly enjoyed these travels and felt the trips were exciting opportunities and rewards for my professional work. My first foreign trips were in 1989, when I traveled to Germany and the Soviet Union, just as *perestroika* was ushering in the free market and sloughing off Cold War policies. It wasn't but two years later that the Soviet Union dissolved. My nine-day visit took me to Moscow, where I was exposed to enough of the inner workings of business practices there to conclude the Cold War was likely melting, but the Soviet economy had yet to recover and begin to heat up.

I was happy because these trips also afforded me an opportunity to work with Harold Norbitz again. Although officially retired from Nathan's, he agreed to accompany me as a consultant for Nathan's. He was helpful during the negotiations with the Russians, our American partner Shelley Zeiger[14], and his company TrenMos. Zeiger had an important relationship with the then mayor of Moscow. Harold personally knew the late Zeiger through other business interactions. Zeiger previously had used his relationships to help American businesses break into the Russian market.

For instance, in 1987 Zeiger was the first to bring pizza to the Soviet Union, and he opened the first American restaurant in Moscow just two years later.[15] His experiences there were vast. On one occasion I remember Zeiger telling us the story about how he had to accept payments in goods, as it was illegal to take rubles out of the country. He ended up accepting Russian nesting dolls for his payments, which he would then export to turn into profit.

The main goal of my Soviet trip was to launch a test with a transportable trailer restaurant, equipped with grills for hot dogs and hamburgers, steam tables, fryers for french fries, and soda dispensers. The trailer also served soup and other products. On the side of the trucks, we painted Nathan's insignia in

---

14  I tried to reach Shelley's son, Jeff, to interview him for this book to obtain additional insights on our brief business relationship with his father, but I was unable to get in touch with him.

15  http://www.trentonian.com/general-news/20131110/trenton-international-businessman-shelley-m-zeiger-dies and http://www.nytimes.com/1987/12/13/nyregion/entrepreneur-to-make-pizzas-in-moscow.html (accessed Dec. 30, 2014).

the Cyrillic alphabet. During this trip, I was also charged with setting up storage for the trailers and teaching the Russian bakery staff how to make hot dog rolls, since we couldn't ship the product there without losing quality.

Since my first order of business was to find a hot dog supplier, my expertise in working with suppliers was critical to this international venture. There was no location in Russia capable of making frankfurters. In fact, companies like McDonald's had to build their own factories. Unfortunately, we did not have the resources or guaranteed business need to build our own. So I attended the annual Anuga Food Fair, the largest food show in the world, held in Cologne, Germany.

While there, I was hopeful to find a supplier who had a relationship with Russia. My hope was to locate a company that would be willing to use our proprietary recipe to manufacture our hot dogs. I figured that because Germany was "wurst" country, I might be able to find a competent supplier there. The food show encompassed 284,000 square meters of display space spread across one square mile, with food exhibitors from all over the world.

Luckily, I did find a manufacturer with a plant in Munich. It seemed like a good idea to change my plans for this trip, so I called our headquarters in New York and suggested that I should go to visit the German plant since I was already overseas. While there, we could discuss our needs, understand this company's capabilities, and see if it had a desire to work with us on this project. Management agreed that my change in plans made sense.

During early discussions with that frank manufacturer, it quickly became apparent that he would not agree to use Nathan's proprietary blend of spices. His company wanted to make the product its way (a blend of pork and beef), without any input or control by us. We obviously couldn't agree to that, as we only use beef in our frankfurters.

With no Russian or European supplier options, the only other opportunity seemed to be shipping frozen hot dogs from the USA to Russia. Doing so was extremely expensive, but we decided to ship Nathan's American manufactured hot dogs in a container via ship, from the Port of Newark, New Jersey, to Helsinki, Finland. We had our representatives go to Helsinki to meet the ship and drive the goods in a truck from Finland to Moscow. This was a better financial option even though it took three to four weeks to get the franks and other products from New Jersey to Moscow.

The Soviets barely had access to many fundamental necessities at the dawn of *perestroika* and *glasnost*, let alone small luxuries. Officially, the Kremlin claimed it had near zero unemployment, but in 1989 the Associated Press reported that about 17 percent of Soviet workers (twenty-three million) were jobless, and in some areas, the rate was 27 percent.[16] Because of shortages of so many essential goods, before I left for Russia I was advised that I should bring cartons of cigarettes, gum, toilet paper, and chocolate. These goods served as gifts instead of money. I gave one of the four or five cartons of cigarettes I'd brought to our driver. I split other cartons and chocolates with everyone else (although I kept some toilet paper for myself, as the hotels only had pretty rough rolls). People liked the cigarettes best. But I did bring soap and candies, which also proved to be popular items as gifts.

I stayed in one of the newest hotels in the center of Moscow, considered to be the most modern and ritzy in the city. But it was more like a mid-priced motel by American and Western standards, with uncomfortable beds and minimal amenities. Even the upscale restaurant in that hotel rarely had meat. On days it served chicken, the locals were eager to dine there, as that was a rare treat. Food shortages plagued the city.

Our translator was a highly educated woman who had just married. Because they wanted to have kids and needed the additional space, she told me that she and her husband were on a two- to three-year waiting list to get a new apartment. They had a car and were both highly skilled and considered very well off, even though they lived in an area where every night they had to take off their windshield wipers and hubcaps from their car or they'd be stolen.

My most memorable time in Moscow was when I taught our Soviet colleagues how to bake rolls. Before I left for Russia, I spent time at our bakery in New York to learn how to do this. To ensure freshness, we knew we had to bake rolls in Russia. The Soviets had large food complexes that housed a dairy,

---

16   http://articles.latimes.com/1989-11-01/business/fi-206_1_soviet-jobless-rate (accessed Dec. 30, 2014).

a slaughterhouse, and a bakery. These were all clustered in one huge area. I was told that two or three such facilities served all of Moscow.

When I first walked through the bakery, I remember thinking that the facility would have to be renovated in order to meet the current codes in the U.S. With these conditions, it was more difficult to make a quality product on a consistent basis. Still, they did their jobs as best they could and took pride in those products that they produced.

In any event, I gave the general manager of the bakery Nathan's roll recipe and worked with him and his people to show them the ropes. I had to explain that our rolls must be light in texture, which requires proofing or letting the dough rise. This concept is a very basic baking principle, but one unfamiliar to them at that time. I offered the formulas, which specified the number of pounds of yeast per hundred pounds of flour, how long to mix the dough with cold water, and how to put the dough into a temperature-controlled proofing box that allows it to rise.

Of course Soviet bakers had yeast, but they only knew how to produce heavy Russian bread. The results of the first test were totally unacceptable. Instead of proofing the dough, the baker had mixed the batter and just cut off a pound of dough and baked it. The rolls came out all wrong. Instead of light and fluffy, they were heavy and doughy. Through my interpreter, I had to explain that proofing would not only improve the quality of the hot dog roll, but would also increase the yield. For instance, if proofed, one pound of dough might produce more rolls than from the same amount of dough without proofing.

The manager of the facility had an epiphany after witnessing the magic of proofing. He looked up and said (through my translator), "Oh my, if I get more product out of the same dough, that means I can get more money." Thus, the miracle of capitalism began to dawn on him.

As he went through mental machinations, I observed him trying to figure out which products he manufactured they could apply the proofing methodology to in order to increase their yields and profit. It was beautiful to behold. I was taking part in something that would assist these people not only to introduce different products to their customers but also to help them understand how to become more profitable.

The rolls came out light and fluffy once we whipped up the batch and trays in accordance with Nathan's recipe. A half dozen bakery workers each tasted a roll. Their eyes lit up as if they were eating Russia's best caviar. One of them commented that it would taste like a dessert if they added sugar. I'm not sure about that, but it was satisfying to see these people enjoy the fruits of their labor.

After this rewarding experience in the bakery, our driver took us back to the office to sign the agreement between TrenMos, Nathan's, and the Moscow mayor's office before we left to go back home.

Accompanying us on this trip was a government representative. I'll never know for sure what government agency he represented, but we got along fine. He was a stocky, dark-haired, bushy eyebrowed man with a quiet personality, but one that warmed up as we got to know one another. In fact, before I got on the plane to leave, he handed me a Russian army watch as a gift of gratitude for my help with the bakery. I truly appreciated this kind gesture. But I consider this watch an emblem of the dysfunction of the Soviet consumer goods industry in 1989. To remind me of my experiences in Russia, I wanted to wear this gift often and for years to come. However, after just two months the watch broke and after several attempts to fix it over twenty-six years later, it sits in my cabinet.

After I returned to the United States on a veritable high, upper Nathan's management poked a hole in my balloon. When I excitedly told them my stories of my visit to Russia, some of them laughed at me. "What, did you have an awakening?" they teased. It was insulting to me because I worked my butt off and felt I had set some positive things in motion. At this point I realized that top management thought of this more as a huge public relations opportunity than a serious business venture. Even though I took my work there seriously, they didn't. This was a wake-up call to me. Obviously this trip was just a promotional idea to generate excitement for the company. It certainly emphasized to me that I would not be a part of determining where the company's growth was going to come from moving forward.

I don't think we earned a dime in Russia with this project. The problem was not that the Soviets rejected our food. As our employees there moved the trailer to different spots they encountered great acceptance of the menu. However, the

Soviet executives and officials made many unfulfilled promises, especially when it came to setting up permanent locations.

After six months, it proved to be an unfruitful project, so we decided to bring our man, Frank Soto Jr., home. He told me he was getting tired and homesick, and there was no real end game in sight. But he did a great job the entire time he was there. He was innovative and quick to react. For example, when the previously shipped food ran out, he would fill the menu with whatever local fare he could scrounge up. But it was time to close our doors after the franks ran out.

Nathan's licensees opened twelve stores in Moscow many years later, which remain there to this day. I wonder whether our trip and all our efforts back in 1989 impacted the decision to invest heavily in the concept.

Despite the chaos *perestroika* caused us, the Zeigers eventually opened a couple of their own independent sit-down restaurants in Russia. Shelley's son, Jeffrey, remained there, offering food to people during the chaos. Looking back, it seems ironic that Americans were able to do business successfully in the Soviet Union for many, many years during Communist rule. In fact, a good number of them made significant money. In the early days of the new "democratic freedom," it became almost impossible to operate.

Still, I am always reminded of this adventure by the poster hanging on my wall that carries the caption: "First Hot Dog in Russia." Whenever I gaze at it, I feel a rush of gratitude and joy for getting the opportunity to experience business in the Soviet Union at such an historic time. I will never forget my trip to Moscow and the people I met and worked with to develop a fast food business in a country that, at the time, would have truly appreciated an American tradition. I have a tremendous amount of respect for the Russian people and specifically for those I had the pleasure of working with during my stay.

But shortly after I returned, I found our company embroiled in a revolution of its own.

## More Trouble in the Executive Suite

Aside from opening a restaurant in Atlanta and in the terminal at Newark International Airport, the new management leadership was not able to produce any better results than the Buckleys had. The leadership changed again and Wayne Norbitz was promoted to president.

After spinning its wheels under two consecutive failed management teams, Nathan's was able to make significant progress with the company's strategic expansion goals, finally realizing some positive financial results. In 1991, and with annual sales of $70 million, Wayne nudged Nathan's beyond the New York area. By 1992, twenty-four of our seventy-nine restaurants and airport outlets were scattered around other parts of the country.

Also, a franchise agreement with Caldor Inc. called for the opening of restaurants in 50 of the retailer's discount stores over the next five years. An agreement was signed to develop Nathan's company owned locations in Home Depot stores. This was financially successful for both partners, but Home Depot later determined that the square footage taken up by restaurants was better served by selling hard goods. So it replaced our in-store restaurants with little local hot dog stands, spanning no more than 150 square feet. Nathan's also inked a third deal, with Bradlees department stores.

The company then began setting its sights (and sites) beyond U.S. borders, with plans to open 185 franchises in Europe and the Far East over the course of the next few years. These plans required a significant new infusion of capital. The company's new leadership decided to look to the public market in 1993, with a public offering of 1.5 million shares priced at $9 per share, raising $13.5 million—less than the amount the company received when Equicor had taken the company private in 1987.

## Back to the Public Market

Going public for a second time proved to be a good move for the company, as well as personally, for many of our management team, as we received some stock options.

Even with that cash infusion, it took a couple of years to return Nathan's to profitability. The company acquired or opened twelve restaurants in the New York region, including some large, full-service outlets that proved costly to build and operate. That may have contributed to fiscal losses in 1995 and 1996, which caused significant dips in the price of the stock.

I was doing my job without the pressure of the previous executive-suite dramas and responsibilities, but I just wasn't happy at work. But I was excited to have another opportunity to travel overseas on behalf of Nathan's.

## Farther East: Japan

In 1993, four years after my trip to the Soviet Union, I was invited to Japan by Fujisankei Communications International Inc., a sponsor of Japan's Live UFO '93, an annual "Golden Week" fourteen-day celebration of the emperor's birthday. Fujisankei wanted me to set up a booth to introduce the Japanese people to Nathan's Famous hot dogs amid the hundreds of vendors in and around Tokyo's street fairs. It was important to the sponsor that I, grandson of the founder, be there, because tradition is everything in Japanese culture. It was a great honor for Nathan's to represent an American company and participate in the festivities.

On a daily basis, we held a hot dog eating contest for fair attendees. The record for wolfing down the most franks was just six or seven, compared with seventeen in the U.S. that same year. We cut down the contests from ten or twelve minutes to six minutes in an attempt to get people to try our product. It was more of a public relations event than a contest. Still, it is quite ironic that in the early twenty-first century, it was Takeru Kobayashi, a Japanese-born contestant, who shattered pretty much every standing record, by wolfing down fifty franks during his first contest. When I first traveled to Japan, the intention of my seventeen-day trip was mostly public relations, but we also hoped to gain exposure to potential partners with whom we could open stores.

Although I did not have to prepare as much for this trip as I had for my Russian travels, I did spend a day with Tracy Steinmetz, a reporter for Fujisankei, who offered me a lesson in Japanese etiquette. She taught me how to address Japanese people and how to present and receive business cards. She also impressed upon me the importance of accepting offered gifts, including food and drinks.

At one meal at the end of the day, my hosts handed me a glass of beer that was more than one foot tall and as wide as a mug. I nurtured that as much as I could, and somehow I managed to finish it, only to find the server returning to replenish my glass. Etiquette aside, I had to put my hand over the mug at that point. I don't know if I insulted him, but I couldn't drink another drop. I was exhausted and ready to drop off to sleep after having been on my feet for more than twelve hours.

Many things about the formality of Japanese culture and the individual respect they showed one another impressed me. For example, there was one occasion when I took the subway and saw three children between four and six years old traveling on their own, carrying backpacks. They were trying to get on the train, probably on their way to school. The transit worker forced the people on the subway car to make room for the children. Everyone on the train moved in to allow them to continue their journey. I was amazed at the respect the busy subway travelers exhibited.

I also saw my share of teens dressed as punk rockers, with black leather attire and spiked colored hair. They acted respectfully toward those around them. They seemed to enjoy the punk style but did not embrace the sullen, rebellious punker attitude.

Fujisankei provided me with a translator who would accompany me to meetings, dinners, and events. We did attend a Japanese ballgame. I was surprised and amused to notice that vendors were selling fish hot dogs at the stadium. Of course I had to try one, but I ended up spitting it out without being noticed; I just could not swallow it, it tasted awful.

At this stadium, instead of cheering or clapping, thousands of people were banging plastic bats together as a way to make noise for their team. The intensity of the sound overwhelmed me, as the banging did not emerge as one chorus in unison, but as a continual syncopated roar. In later years, Nathan's made some of these bats and handed them out to the audience at our annual hot dog eating contests in Coney Island.

I found that Japanese businesspeople worked extremely hard. Most mornings at eight o'clock, my translator met me downstairs for breakfast meetings, with our days ending at 9 p.m. He would commute more than an hour each way to the city and worked so hard during these two weeks that he fell asleep during our attendance at the baseball game. I decided we should leave before the end of the game so he could return to his family and get some much deserved rest.

My 1993 trip did attract plenty of publicity, which was after all the main purpose of my expedition. In fact, while I was there I appeared on CNN to discuss our global expansion. I was flabbergasted when a friend of mine in Switzerland called to say he had seen that interview.

During my hectic seventeen days in Japan, I only found two hours to myself to do any sightseeing. I spent that time visiting a Buddhist temple, so not all was lost. After returning home from Japan, and about a year after the Live UFO experience, Wayne asked me to become vice president of operations. I was very appreciative of the offer and knew that I was more than qualified to do the job. I had the respect of our entire operations team for my hard work. But I had other ideas.

After much consideration, as well as a lengthy discussion with my wife, Amy, I declined the job opportunity. I was familiar with the job responsibilities and didn't want the stress or long hours at that time in my life. I felt that I could do a better job continuing in my position in corporate food service and public relations work. However, declining the promotion may have triggered the end of my days at Nathan's.

*Frank Soto Jr. (extreme left) William Handwerker (center)*
*Aaron Schaffel (extreme right) with local workers in Tokyo, 1993*
*Photo Credit: Handwerker Family collection*

> **Frank Lesson:** *Know your capabilities, limitations, and long-term goals. Sometimes the best opportunity is the one we decline.*

## The End of My Road at Nathan's

I was not a happy camper by the time 1996 rolled around. I can't put a finger on exactly why, but I knew that I had to leave the company and try something else. I would leave work depressed. As the last remaining Handwerker at Nathan's, I realized I was very conflicted about leaving the company. I was forty-four and still had many working years ahead of me. What would I do next? That was of little concern at the time. I just knew one thing: I had to leave.

My son was going to become a Bar Mitzvah that year, and I intended to wait until after the celebration to let Wayne know I was leaving the company. Little did I know that Wayne and the company had other plans for the end of my career.

> **Frank Lesson:** *No matter how much you plan and believe you are in control, life often has other plans for you.*

Wayne invited me to lunch at a local restaurant one day in the spring of that year. I can only guess that he chose a public place to minimize the chance of an emotional outburst when he told me, "We have to let you go." But he obviously did not expect my reaction: I started to smile. I had been miserable for the prior six months. The job felt routine. Maybe Wayne was right to have asked me to take that promotion to vice president of operations. I may not have felt so bored had I accepted the offer.

Still, I had such mixed feelings. On the one hand, it was difficult for me to take the initiative to quit and let go of my connection to my legacy, and then accept that there would be no more Handwerkers at the company. On the other hand, it was a relief when Wayne essentially made the decision for me, allowing me to get paid to leave instead of quitting, with no severance pay or benefits. So we negotiated a mutually acceptable package.

To this day, I am proud of my almost thirty years at the company—from the time I was thirteen years old behind the counter serving fries in Coney Island to becoming a married adult with two kids. After the sale in 1987, the fact that the company kept me on for nine years was indicative of the substantial value I provided it.

I prepared a memo to management before I packed up my office and handed over the keys. It outlined my personal views regarding the substantial reasons for the company's problems at the time, as well as my vision of how the company might best proceed to achieve long-term, sustainable success.

I still have the sheet with bullet points outlining that memo. It states that some of the obstacles at the time were: pricing ourselves out of the traditional restaurant marketplace, an inability to compete with major chains' advertising budgets, a negative health image of hot dogs that dragged down sales of franks throughout the industry, and rundown, old company restaurant facilities.

> **Frank Lesson:** *Always take an opportunity to leave a lasting impression and take the "high road." In the future, you never know who you will be dealing with and under what circumstances.*

In hindsight, I wasn't completely right. I recognize now that I was wrong about pricing. To date, the company pricing of the frank and fries are definitively accepted by the consuming public. They met the basic precepts of perceived value to the customer base. But the advertising budget issue still remains. However, they have been able to carve a niche in the marketing arena with the hot dog eating contest and all the hoopla it welcomes. They implement local campaigns to endear themselves to various localities around the country with the "Kaboom" program, where they assist in the building of kids' playgrounds through the great expense and efforts of John Morrell & Co.

As far as health issues are concerned, my father had an expression that holds true: "Everything in moderation!" Americans enjoy their food, and when someone wants to have a hot dog every so often, they want the best, and that's a Nathan's frankfurter!

In addition to my list of concerns, my suggestions for the future included: focusing on our growing supermarket program; selling franks to potential customers by the pound; trying to acquire a meat production facility; setting up a marketing plan for institutional hot dog sales programs; developing prepared french fries that could be used in smaller restaurants such as at convenience stores with no preparation space; addressing franchisee concerns about how to compete with the licensing program; expanding the supermarket sales to include Nathan's branded fries, sauerkraut, mustard, pickles, cheese sauce, and chips; more aggressively pursuing overseas expansion of franchises; and renovating the long-neglected flagship restaurant in Coney Island.

I can't help but feel gratified that whether or not my memo provided the impetus, the company ended up pursuing many of the initiatives I recommended, and that Nathan's, as of this writing, has enjoyed many subsequent years of growth in both sales and profits.

> **Frank Lesson:** *Nothing is more important than your legacy. Remember that what you do today will impact how you are perceived tomorrow.*

## Chapter 10

# New Beginnings and Endings

*A*fter leaving Nathan's, I wanted to create a sit-down restaurant like my father had done in Oceanside more than forty years earlier. I envisioned opening a venue with mid-priced food similar to that of Nathan's former sit-down restaurant. One idea was to bring barbecue ribs to New York. I even approached the attorney for a barbecue franchise in Washington, DC. They were not interested in expanding beyond their comfort zone in the South and Southwest. In retrospect, I was ahead of my time and couldn't get it done in a manner that made me feel comfortable.

Instead, in 1998 I found an investment in a sit-down restaurant concept that excited me. I joined the private investment group as executive vice president and was charged with negotiating a multimillion-dollar international agreement to license the name "Sporting News" to open restaurants that would also market memorabilia. I got involved with developing this concept on a national and international basis. I truly loved the idea of expanding upon a brand that had a great past, like Nathan's. In the late 90's, themed restaurants were very popular. I felt that I could combine my experience in licensing and restaurant franchising with my love for sports. Unfortunately, things did not work out as we expected.

For years I had been managing my own family's financial matters. In 2001, I became an investment advisor representative, and I currently work at Lincoln Financial Advisors, where I specialize in financial planning for business owners, their employees, and for individuals.

Now, as I look back at the family business through the lens of my subsequent experiences as an entrepreneur in my own right, I feel a renewed sense of appreciation for all that my grandfather and father accomplished. Even though I have moved on, I feel connected to Nathan's, its rich history, and its bright future. It is deep-seated and will remain a part of the fabric of my being for as long as I live. In fact, I still get a warm feeling every time I walk by a Nathan's restaurant.

## The End of Generation Two

Murray spent the last years of his life dealing with the effects of dementia caused by several mini-strokes called TIAs. These medical ailments weighed heavily on our whole family, especially my mom. Sadly, those enduring dementia's debilitating effects are usually not the ones who suffer most. Even though the family hired constant outside care for him, Dorothy would not hear of leaving his side. She would rarely, if at all, leave the apartment.

Amy was often on the phone while my mother cried about her experience with my father. My brother Steve became the primary caregiver of our parents and would constantly go to the apartment to take care of things that needed to be done on a regular basis. He tried to convince her to go out and enjoy a few hours off with friends. But it was to no avail. My other brother, Ken, would visit with them as much as he could to help bring some happiness during their last years. Amy and I often discussed how this lifestyle may kill my mother first. Sadly, we were right.

In June 2009, my mother died at age eighty-six. She passed away from a brain hemorrhage at her home in Florida, where she and my father lived. While she never actively worked at the company, my father (and I) valued her opinions and input about Nathan's. After she influenced Murray to retire in 1987, they enjoyed the last twenty-two of their sixty-seven married years together by attending local university classes, playing golf, and visiting with friends and family. Unfortunately, the last five years together were not what they had planned.

After her death, and because of his dementia, my dad would still ask for her even though he understood she was gone. When I spoke with Murray, he would occasionally ask me about Coney Island and the store. I would tell him that I still spoke with Wayne, Bruce Miller (senior director of operations), and Samantha Sugrim (general manager of the Coney Island restaurant) every now and then, and they would tell me about the progress of Coney Island. He would smile whenever we spoke about Coney. It was clear that these were the most relevant memories he retained. I would always talk about going to the store and how wonderful Coney Island was in those days. He enjoyed these conversations greatly, even to the end.

Through the years, we spoke on the phone less often, since he did not have the strength to hold the receiver. Even though I don't think he knew we were there, those last visits with him were extremely important to each of us. I was so sad every time I left his apartment, and told my family this current condition was a terrible way to end a long and productive life. The only thing my brothers and I could do was keep him comfortable until his death.

In 2011, I wanted to do something special for Murray's ninetieth birthday. The idea was to bring him back to Coney Island for one last visit. My brother's agreed that the trip would be a wonderful thing for him. We all understood that the trip could be dangerous but decided what good is living without some happiness every now and again? We investigated various ways to bring him up to New York as comfortably and safely as possible.

Unfortunately, Murray followed my mother before his birthday, leaving this world at age eighty-nine, after succumbing to the complications of dementia. The legacy he created as the head of a growing family business that became an international household name cannot be overstated. He and my mother were also wonderful parents and grandparents, who lived and imparted meaningful values on all those around them.

Many months before my mom's death, she took me aside and emphatically requested that I do something when Murray passed. She gave me an impassioned plea to make sure that Murray's obituary told the story of how he built Nathan's throughout his years as the head of the company, his great pride in his accomplishments, and how much he loved Coney Island. All who knew him never doubted this fact.

I called Mortimer Matz, who is still actively working even into his nineties, to help me secure a nice obituary for Murray. He did a great job, and I received several calls from reporters throughout the country, asking me to tell Murray's story again and again. I knew that my mom would be content to know that he got the recognition he deserved for the success and his role in Nathan's.

Before he was laid to rest, there was one last thing I had to do for my dad. After Nathan passed away in 1974, I vividly remember my grandfather's funeral procession going past the Coney Island store. I felt so strongly that Murray deserved the same recognition and respect that was bestowed upon Nathan. So, Amy and I went to the airport with the funeral home people to pick up my father's body from the flight from Florida. I much appreciated the support that my children Michael, Adam and Franny showed when they came out to Coney Island to be with us for the small gathering and make the toast to my dad.

I called Bruce Miller to let him know that we were coming to the store. Samantha, the general manager, and an old employee who knew my dad and still worked there, greeted us when we stopped in front of the store. I asked for a plate of hot dogs so we could toast my dad one last time. I took the hot dog and said, "Here's to you, Pop, may you rest in peace." I knew he would be very happy that he had this last chance to visit the store.

## Success and Legacy

I have been out of the business since 1996, but my feelings about Nathan's Famous are still strong and run through my blood. So much so that whenever I go into a Nathan's restaurant or smaller imprint, my curiosity is still piqued to find out the inner workings of that store. Are the franks hot? Are the rolls warm, dry, or stale? I can't stop myself. I've been out of the business for close to twenty years, but I still call up the company and let them know if I see something I feel needs to be addressed to preserve the integrity of the brand. I still view it as my family legacy.

I learned a lot about my family legacy through working closely with Murray, as well as my brother Kenny. Unfortunately, I had limited time with my grandfather in the day-to-day operations as a child working in Coney Island. However, all of these opportunities allowed me to hear about my heritage and legacy from the horse's mouth. This intimate knowledge and firsthand experience was truly amazing and eye opening. I couldn't be more thankful for being a part of my family's restaurant history.

But it wasn't just about a journey through Nathan's. I learned remarkable lessons about business and life from my wise grandfather, father, and many nonfamily executives and operations line personnel. These lessons and stories comprise the most valuable inheritance I received.

Working with family members can be challenging. There are many stories about dysfunctional situations that fester and sometimes destroy relationships at other family companies, both large and small. As I've described, my own family had its share of these same squabbles and tensions. But we continue to work well together on any family issues that still arise, inside and outside the company.

Today the company is stronger than ever. Nathan's has 238 stores in 43 states in the USA and 39 stores in 8 countries, with more international

*Nathan's worldwide locations*
*Photo Credit: Nathan's Famous website*

expansion to come. I'm impressed and delighted that current management has continued to propel the company to new heights and unforeseen opportunities. I feel gratified that the company continues to renovate stores, especially the flagship Coney Island location, which was rebuilt after Hurricane Sandy devastated it in 2012.

All of the first three stores, Coney Island, Oceanside, and Yonkers, remain successful to this day. All three locations reflect the most up-to-date industry customer service and design features. Countless numbers of people I have met over the years have told me about their fun-filled experiences at all three of the original restaurants: the ones that ultimately met their wives at Coney Island, the ones that went to Oceanside every Friday night and Saturday after their high school football or basketball games, or to Yonkers and their huge game room with their kids. They always had big smiles on their faces while telling me of their fond memories. I would say to the people who went to Oceanside, "I probably served you!" and that I have the same great memories as well.

These three stores were only the start of Murray's dream. Clearly, if Nathan had not allowed Murray to expand beyond the original Coney Island store, take the company public, and establish franchising and licensing programs, Nathan's Famous would hardly be as famous and recognized as it is today.

I am excited to say that the current management team has brought the company to new heights. They understand the goals of what Murray and I desired and have made them a reality. I think my father, grandfather and grandmother would be proud that the company they worked so hard to sustain and grow is celebrating its one hundredth anniversary as this book hits bookstore shelves in 2016. With that said, here's to the next hundred years of success!

As important as the future, continued success of Nathan's is, I want this book to be a reminder to my children, grandchildren, and future generations of the Handwerker family of what their ancestors were able to accomplish. If they set out from the start with the same fortitude to accomplish their goals, whatever they may be, they will also achieve success. Persevere, and good things will happen!

In conclusion, I am still trying to adhere to the axioms in Mother Teresa's poem and fulfill the wonders of life and all that it holds. Don't sit back and observe; be a participant. Both happy and sad events happen to us all as part of our time here on Earth. We should learn from both and move forward.

*Poster of Nathan and Ida inducted into the*
*Coney Island Hall of Fame/Coney Island History Project*

# About the Author

**William Handwerker** is the grandson of Nathan Handwerker, founder of America's favorite frankfurter company and the iconic Coney Island, New York institution. Working alongside his grandfather and father, Murray, for 30 years, William penned *Nathan's Famous The First 100 Years...* to commemorate the enormous entrepreneurial spirit of his grandfather's legacy and the business history of one of America's most loved foods— the Nathan's Famous frankfurter. He worked as a teenager at the Coney Island and Oceanside restaurants during summers, weekends, and holidays. After graduating from Ithaca College, William joined his family's company fulltime in 1976.

During his tenure with the company, William spearheaded operational improvements in the chain's supply distribution methodology, product cooking processes, supermarket licensing program, and promotional and marketing campaigns including judging the early years of the Nathan's Famous Hotdog Eating Contests. William, who rose to Senior Vice President of Corporate Foodservice, departed the company in 1996. William has been interviewed by

CNN, the Food Network, the History Channel, and numerous national and New York media.

Since leaving the company he still maintains a relationship with the Coney Island community through the efforts of The Coney Island Alliance organization. He has been involved with a variety of charitable organizations over the years and intends on pursuing future involvement as personal time and opportunities arise.

William has been in the financial investment industry for the past fifteen years and currently is an Investment Advisor Representative at Lincoln Financial Advisors.

**Jayne Pearl** is a journalist and entertaining speaker, focusing on family business and financial parenting. She is also co-author (with Richard Morris) of *Kids, Wealth and Consequences: Ensuring a Responsible Financial Future for the Next Generation* (John E. Wiley, 2010) and has co-authored or ghost-written nineteen other books. Jayne began her career at *Forbes* and was former senior editor of *Family Business* magazine, to which she has contributed for more than 20 years. She has written hundreds of articles about family business, financial parenting, personal finance and business management. She has also appeared on PBS, CNBC's *Power Lunch*, NPR and CNN, and been quoted in publications such as the *Inc., Washington Post, Washington Times, Christian Science Monitor, Reuters, Forbes, Scholastic* magazine, *Parenting, Real Simple, Working Mother* and *US News & World Report.*

Printed in the USA
CPSIA information can be obtained
at www.ICGtesting.com
JSHW022333140824
68134JS00019B/1462

9 781630 479343